Michael Snow
Wavelength

Elizabeth Legge

One Work Series Editor
Mark Lewis

Afterall Books Editors
Charles Esche and Mark Lewis

Managing Editor
Pablo Lafuente

Associate Editor
Melissa Gronlund

Copy Editor
Deirdre O' Dwyer

Picture Editor
Gaia Alessi

Other titles in the *One Work* series:

Bas Jan Ader: In Search of the Miraculous
by Jan Verwoert

Hollis Frampton: (nostalgia)
by Rachel Moore

*Ilya Kabakov: The Man Who Flew
into Space from his Apartment*
by Boris Groys

Richard Prince: Untitled (couple)
by Michael Newman

*Joan Jonas: I Want to Live in the Country
(And Other Romances)*
by Susan Morgan

*Mary Heilmann: Save the Last
Dance for Me*
by Terry R. Myers

*Marc Camille Chaimowicz:
Celebration? Realife*
by Tom Holert

Yvonne Rainer: The Mind is a Muscle
by Catherine Wood

Fischli and Weiss: The Way Things Go
by Jeremy Millar

Andy Warhol: Blow Job
by Peter Gidal

Alighiero e Boetti: Mappa
by Luca Cerizza

*Hanne Darboven: Cultural History
1880–1983*
by Janet Harbord

Chris Marker: La Jetée
by Janet Harbord

Sarah Lucas: Au Naturel
by Amna Malik

One Work is a unique series of books published by Afterall, based
at Central Saint Martins College of Art and Design in London.
Each book presents a single work of art considered in detail by
a single author. The focus of the series is on contemporary art
and its aim is to provoke debate about significant moments in
art's recent development.

Over the course of more than one hundred books, important works
will be presented in a meticulous and generous manner by writers
who believe passionately in the originality and significance of the
works about which they have chosen to write. Each book contains
a comprehensive and detailed formal description of the work,
followed by a critical mapping of the aesthetic and cultural context
in which it was made and has gone on to shape. The changing
presentation and reception of the work throughout its existence
is also discussed, and each writer stakes a claim on the influence
'their' work has on the making and understanding of other
works of art.

The books insist that a single contemporary work of art (in all
of its different manifestations), through a unique and radical
aesthetic articulation or invention, can affect our understanding
of art in general. More than that, these books suggest that a single
work of art can literally transform, however modestly, the way
we look at and understand the world. In this sense the *One Work*
series, while by no means exhaustive, will eventually become
a veritable library of works of art that have made a difference.

First published in 2009
by Afterall Books

Afterall
Central Saint Martins
College of Art and Design,
University of the Arts London,
107–109 Charing Cross Road,
London WC2H ODU
www.afterall.org

ISBN Paperback: 978–1–84638–056–3
ISBN Cloth: 978–1–84638–055–6

Distribution by The MIT Press,
Cambridge, Massachusetts and London
www.mitpress.mit.edu

Art Direction and Typeface Design
A2/SW/HK

Printed and bound by
Die Keure, Belgium

The *One Work* series is printed
on FSC certified papers

Images of work by Michael Snow are courtesy the artist.

The stills of *Wavelength* reproduced in this book are accompanied by the optical
soundtrack (on the right of each image). This is to demonstrate the way the sound
changes, in relation to the zoom, throughout the film. We are grateful to the author
and the University of Toronto for providing these images.

The artist's notes reproduced in this book are held at the Snow archive /
Fonds Snow (FS) Art Gallery of Ontario, E.P. Taylor Research Library and Archives.
Each document is listed by box number followed by file number.

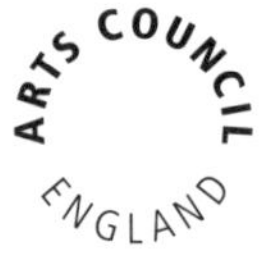

Michael Snow
Wavelength

Elizabeth Legge

My thanks to Larry Pfaff and Amy Marshall at the E.P. Taylor
Research Library & Archives, Art Gallery of Ontario, Toronto;
Liz Dobson, Nina Kurtovic and Jann Marson for their work
in the archives; and Steven R. Taylor, the Video Film Archivist
at Ogilvy & Mather, New York, for his informed discussion of
advertising in the 1960s. Michael Fried invited me to give seminars
on Michael Snow at Johns Hopkins University, and I am indebted
to him in equal measure for his eagle-eyed ferocity and his
intellectual generosity. To Michael Snow and Peggy Gale,
Prospero's apposite promise: 'I'll deliver all; / And promise you
calm seas, auspicious gales...' (William Shakespeare, *The Tempest*,
Act V, Scene 1)

Elizabeth Legge has written on Dada, Surrealism and
contemporary art, especially with respect to the ways visual
artists work with and against language, and the instrumental
uses of stereotypes, in journals including *Art History, Word and
Image* and *Representations*. Recent publications include the book
Editing the Image (co-edited with Mark Cheetham and Catherine
M. Soussloff, University of Toronto Press, 2008) and '*Faire de
son histoire une boucle (noire)*: Ways of Looking at Tristan Tzara',
Art History, vol. 32, no.1 (February 2009).

This essay about a beautiful film is in memory of friends
Jane Elizabeth Martin (1950–1981) and
Mary Elisabeth Goforth Jeffrey (1951–2008).

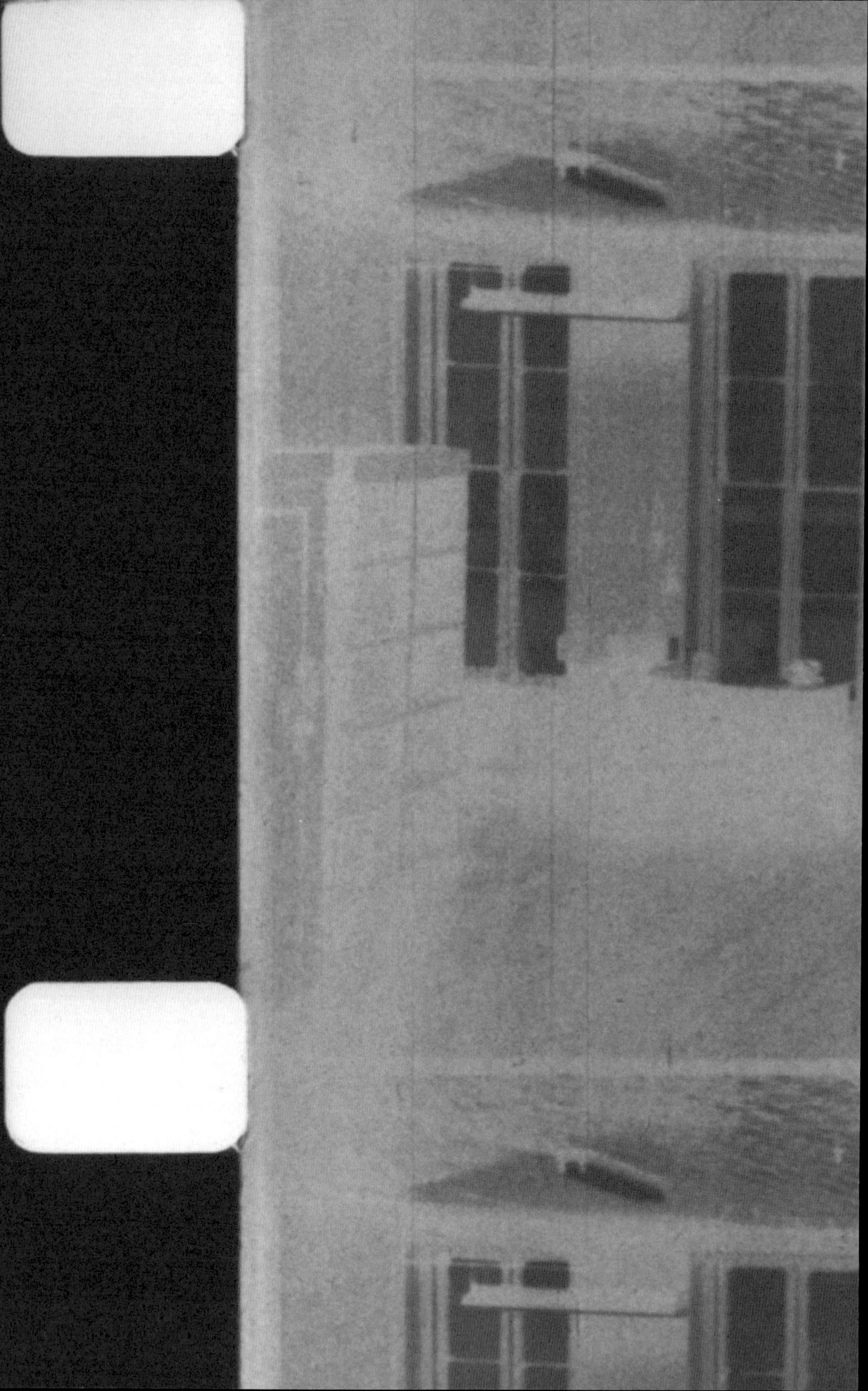

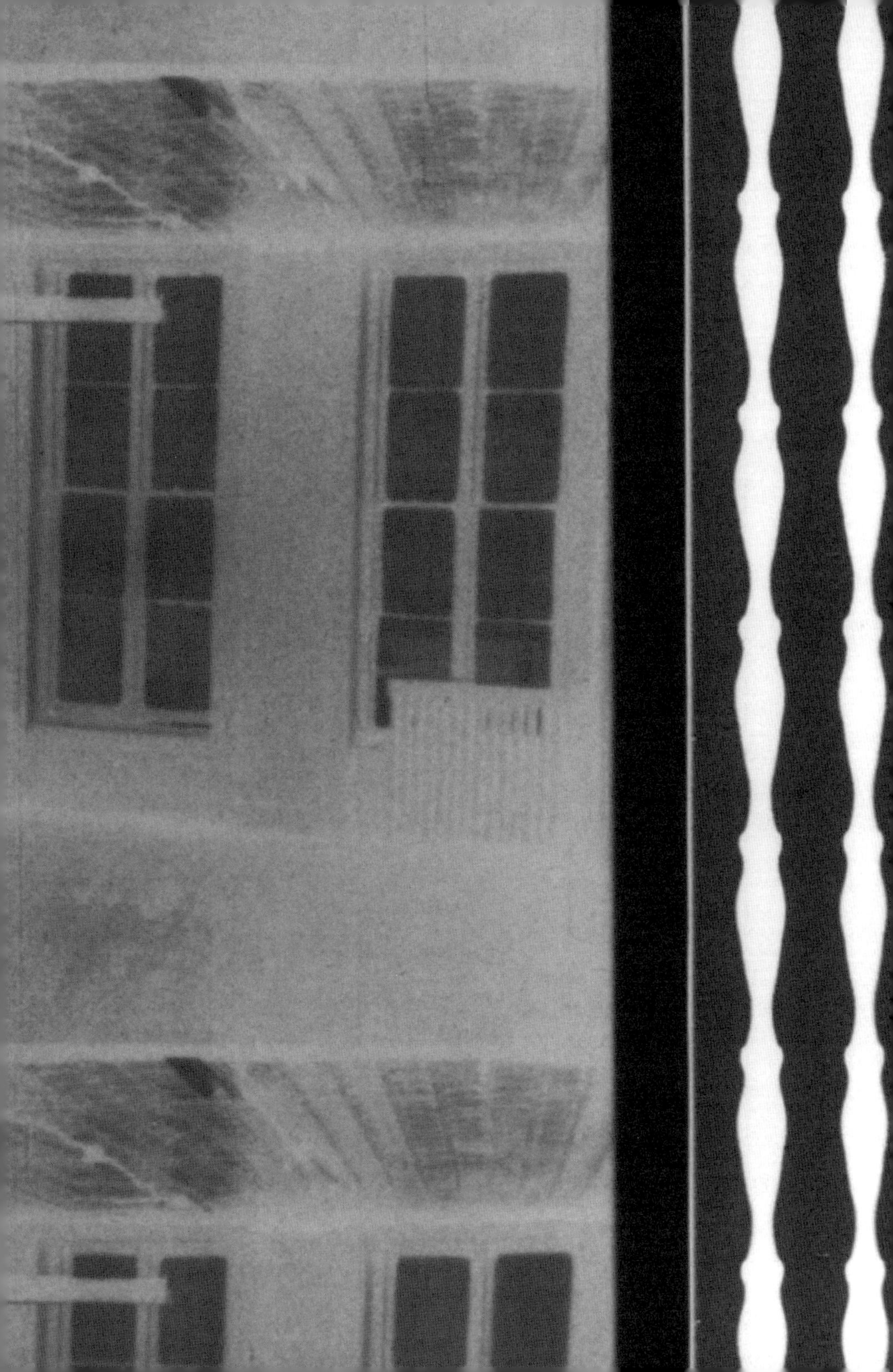

cover and previous pages

Michael Snow,
Wavelength, 1966—67,
16mm colour film,
45min, optical soundtrack detail
and filmstrip detail

*Wavelength was shot in one week in Dec '66 preceded by a year
of notes, thots, mutterings. It was edited and first print seen in
May '67. I wanted to make a summation of my nervous system,
religious inklings and aesthetic ideas. I was thinking of, planning
for, a time monument in which the beauty and sadness of equivalence
would be celebrated, thinking of, trying to, make a definitive
statement of pure film space and time, a balancing of 'illusion' and
'fact', all about seeing. The space starts at the camera's (spectator's)
eye, is in the air, then is on the screen, then is within the screen
(the mind). The film is a continuous zoom which takes 45 minutes
to go from its widest field to its smallest and final field. It was
shot with a fixed camera from one end of an 80-foot loft, shooting
the other end, a row of windows and the street. This, the setting,
and the action which takes place there are cosmically equivalent.
The room (and the zoom) are interrupted by 4 human events
including a death. The sound on these occasions is sync sound,
music and speech, occurring simultaneously with an electronic
sound, a sine wave, which goes from its lowest (50 cycles per second)
to its highest (12,000) in 40 minutes. It is a total glissando while
the film is a crescendo and a dispersed spectrum which attempts
to utilize the gifts of both prophecy and memory which only film
and music have to offer.*[1]
— Michael Snow, 1967

Room Zoom Sine Wave

In 1966, at the height of Minimalist art and its objects, Michael
Snow, a Canadian artist, film-maker and musician then living
in New York, chose not to make another object to be placed in
a room, but instead planned a film *of* a room. In his extensive
notes, consisting of permutative word constellations dispersed
over pages that Snow describes as musings about a possible title,
sometimes circled or underlined, the patterns create visual
rhythms like a notation of waves: 'Atlantic room, Atlantic room
time, ocean room, room time, room tide, room removal, in the

room, in a room … ocean room … wave trip … wet room …
wavelength room … wave room … wavelength … room length …
room wavelength … wave room…'.[2] Gradually, the notes about
a room consolidate as scores for the various qualities and phases
of a zoom. The film, which began in the notes as 'zoom film',
was developed into *Wavelength*, a 45-minute zoom in more or
less a straight line to the far wall of a loft space, with the
accompaniment of a rising sine wave. *Wavelength* has functioned
ever since as a touchstone for contemporary art and film studies,
and as a blue screen in front of which a range of ideological and
intellectual dramas have been played.

The film begins in silence with a yellow field of colour, followed
by a few seconds of a saturated red. There is an abrupt shift to
loud traffic sounds and a scene of a large empty room. The camera
takes a raised point of view, making the expanse of floorboards
of the loft stretch away steeply, like the raked floor of a stage.
Immediately, a woman in a red coat walks on and directs two
men carrying bookshelves. They place them against the left
wall, creating the sense of a stage being set and, consequently,
the expectation of incident to follow (fig.1).[3] The far wall is
composed of four tall, mullioned windows, proportioned and
spaced in a way that casts the enduring spell of classicism on the
tin-ceilinged industrial space. In addition to the shelves, there
are a few furnishings and objects, placed by a side wall and at the
far end of the empty space, including a radiator, a wooden swivel
chair in front of a desk with a radio, a black telephone, a bright
white piece of paper, a clock and, in the middle, between two
windows, a bright yellow vinyl kitchen chair with three images
casually tacked on the wall above it. (The yellow chair and the
woman's red coat appear as the embodied versions of the opening
abstract passages of yellow and red.) This could be the last
clerical outpost of a defunct business, but the function of the
room isn't exactly clear. There is no paraphernalia typical of an

AREA CODE

ROOM TREAT   HEAT AND SAVE
Room
HEAVEN ROOM   WE ONLY LOOK
ATLANTIC ROOM   Room   ROOM ROOM ROOM
                                 RAILROAD FLAT
          STAY IN YOUR ROOM
                                    Trip Room
ZOOM FLAT   LOFT WAVE
20   Radio Room   COAT
Valley Room   FREQUENT ROOM   Ro
Seldom   SPECTRUM   SEA TRANT
        BEGINNING and ENDIN   Room DIAL
   CLEAR ROOM   Room   Room soon
Room   PACKED ROOM   ROOM GLISSANDO

EVERYTHING that goes on   This room is bugged
ATLANTIC SLEEVE ROOM   ALONG ROOM
       ROOM LEGS   HEAT WAVE
ROOM AND OUT   AMY'S ROOM
HAIR CUT   SNOW ROOM   WINDOWS
  HOLY ROOM DATA   LOFT
   WINDOWED W   EYES ROOM WAVES
DIAL ROOM   Room
  SIGHT ROOM   SEEING ROOM

                    AREA   TIME CLOCKS

      PARTS
             INTERIOR WAVES

Michael Snow,
sample of notes, 1966.
FS box no.11, file no.2

40 minute film (roughly)
100' equals 3 minute   = 14 rolls film

ROLLS

1
2   BRING IN BOOKCASE   just one maybe color thing
                                      flash fried
3   slow color changes
4   Slow color changes YELLOWS mostly

5   MAN DIES   at least
6   color changes increase in excitement   4 rolls of
7   8,9, part of 10 flashback   "correct" film
8   ORANGE
9   (Zoom passes body (takes about 15 minutes)   REDS

10
11   AMY PHONES   ) purples
                                              Blues mostly
                                                greens
12
13   zoom reaches and frames photo end of
                        roll 13 and thru 14
14   correct film for indoor not sunlight

Put one slight maybe color action
color this in the parts   dont forget lab mixes
                          from roll to roll

EARLY MORNING

Michael Snow,
sample of notes, 1966.
FS box no.11, file no.2

artist's studio, as had been reverentially or ironically staged
in photo-essays by artists such as Rudy Burckhardt.[4] Snow was
certainly aware of the potential staginess of the typical artist's
studio: 'Look around you in your studio. What does it all mean?
Isn't it corny? The question, I mean. Maybe I mean it all too.'[5]

The camera slowly zooms into the far wall, punctuated by what
Snow laconically refers to as '4 human events':[6] the two men
install the shelves as directed by the woman in the red coat;
the woman comes in again later with another woman, and
they casually perch and drink from mugs while listening to
The Beatles's song 'Strawberry Fields Forever' (1967) on the radio
(fig.2); after protracted crashing and shattering noises, a man
walks in, wheels around and drops dead (fig.8—11); and, lastly,
a young woman comes into the room and, frightened, makes
a telephone call reporting the dead man: 'And he doesn't look
drunk, he looks dead!' (fig.14). Her slightly whispery, caught
voice adds a touch of *film noir* exoticism to the overall tone of the
film. These 'human' events, humdrum or melodramatic, play
against medium-focused fluctuations in stock, slight shifts in
the zoom, positive-negative reversals, monochromatic episodes
and passages of intense saturated colour that flood the image.
The first two events, with the movers and women entering as
if from in front of the screen and retreating into it, mark out
the deep space of the room as it would be traversed by human
movement; but the rest of the film abstracts that space, making
it incrementally more shallow and flat with each phase of the
zoom. Projected, the human events are transmuted into light,
and thus become 'more equivalent' to every other filmed thing.
Snow's phrase '4 human events', perhaps a nod to Fluxus artists'
'event scores', implies that everything else is also an event,
though of another kind: the passages of light and colour that
accelerate to a near strobing effect as if they were a pathetic
fallacy in electromagnetic form, anticipating and doubling the

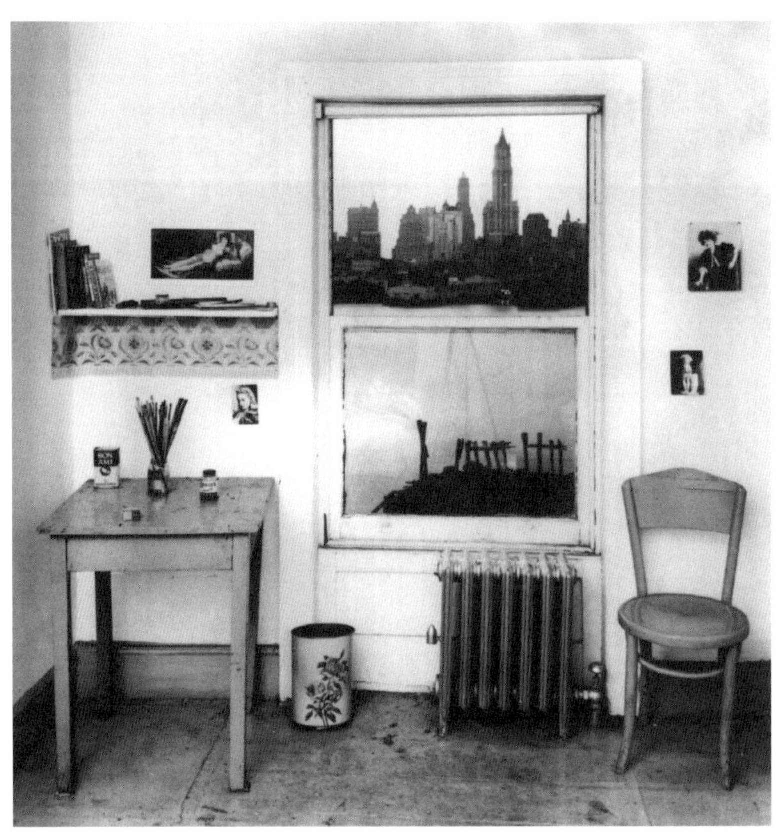

Rudy Burckhardt,
A View from Brooklyn I, 1953,
gelatin silver print, © ARS,
New York and DACS, London, 2009

man's death, are also events.[7] Another sort of event occurs
when the screen image intermittently superimposes images,
in a slight double vision, as if the camera lens or projector
were malfunctioning, or as if our eyes were mis-seeing (fig.15).
There is a feeling that what we are being shown is analogous
to our own vision, reinforced by the fact that the sudden flares
of light, caused by the overexposing of the ends of film when
loading it, resemble blinks meant to clear tired vision — as
if the room itself were an eye. In any case, the resolved screen
image gives way to a bleary caution about our binocular vision.

The film shows a beautiful play of the qualities of light, which
Snow had envisioned from the outset: 'Sunny day, sun shines
on buildings opposite beautiful at 2:00 afternoon.'[8] Light falls
in angled bars through the slats of the radiator and mullioned
windowpanes, glazes the shiny tin ceiling (where it seems
liquid, as opposed to its powdery patterns on the wooden floor),
is framed by the windows as cold daylight against the relative
artificial light and shadow in the room, or casts a fluorescent
pallor against the black windows at night. Sometimes the
windows frame store signs and the tops of passing trucks and
pedestrians in the street; at other times adjustments in exposure
bleach the windowpanes until their radiant whiteness leeches
away the solid window frames; at still others the panes turn
as black as a chalkboard. In sections where Snow uses expired
stock, the image is bleached and bathed in a slightly grainy warm
whiteness, like blindness in a white-out. The light flutters,
rinses, flashes and sifts with changing intensity and textures,
at one point turning the yellow vinyl chair and the wall behind
it golden (fig.3). In one passage of negative reversal, the pools
of shadow at the base of the windows, on top of the suspended
light fixtures and around the desk are reversed to white, and
transformed into accumulations of something bright but material, as if dust had become snow (a leitmotif for Snow) (fig.4).

Almost nine minutes in, the representational image and sounds
of the room cut out to a silent red screen for several seconds,
which then gives way to a murky gloom from which the room
re-emerges, now accompanied by the strange sound of a rising
sine wave, a mechanically generated primal sound that can be
as much felt as heard. The sine wave takes over from the boomy
live sounds of the footsteps in the room and the rumbling traffic
outside, which are also experienced as sounds within the room.
The buzzer-like keening of the sine wave begins to assert itself
at a point when the filmed image seems to become unstable,
marking a new phase of the zoom, lapsing into passages of
negative monochromatic colour or just blank whiteness —
for example, at 11:40 minutes the screen goes white for 20
seconds. As with the light, there are different valences of sound:
a moment when one of the women shuts a window and the street
noises are briefly blanked out (an 'optical effect of silence');[9]
passages when the sine wave alone is heard in its progress
from a low buzzer sound to shrill drilling; and passages when
it in turn seems to be overridden by the crashing noises or the
telephone call. There is in *Wavelength* a fluctuating tension
between abstraction (the sine wave and the passages of solid
colour) and the representational (the sync sound relating to
the filmed room).

For his previous film, *New York Eye and Ear Control* (1964),
Snow recorded the free jazz of the soundtrack and filmed the
images without reference to one another, a strategy that tested
the limits of the medium of film by not taking them as limitations but as infinitely adaptable resources. If the sine wave
might seem like the inflexible opposite to free jazz, in fact
its rise, although apparently set on a predetermined course,
also works in unexpected ways with the image and sync sounds.
Eventually, the sine wave glissando seems to reach its own
limits, and toward the high end of its register it shreds off into

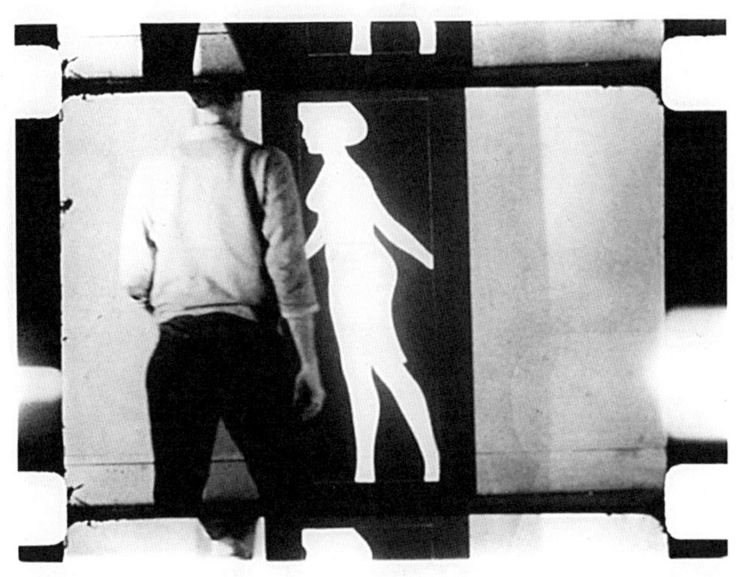

Michael Snow,
New York Eye and Ear Control, 1964,
16mm black-and-white film,
34min, still

a mechanical ululation of sirens, right before moving beyond the
auditory range of the optical soundtrack into silence. Snow has
explained that these siren sounds are an effect of the instabilities
in the interaction of the sine wave generator and the tape
recording.[10] Intentionality may have played a part — he jotted
in his notes 'noises in street like sirens' and 'sirens after radio
shut off'[11] — although Snow's notes point not only to the ideas
that he included in *Wavelength* but also to what he chose not to
do in the film.

At first, the camera zoom seems to be headed toward a square of
open window; yet later it assumes an increasingly oblique angle,
veering slightly left, drawing, as it were, a narrow 'X' against
the orientation of the floorboards. After about thirteen minutes
it seems possible that the zoom is directed toward the three dark
images above the yellow chair, but that does not become certain
until the last fifteen minutes, partly because the images remain
murky for so long: for a great part of the film, we cannot make
them out. At the top is a double magazine photograph of a woman
seen walking toward the camera in one image and away in
another, but the photograph never really comes into focus.[12]
Beneath are two overlapping white silhouettes of the 'walking
woman' figure that had been the principal motif in Snow's
earlier work, which only come into focus in the last fifteen
minutes. The doubling of these images of women echoes increa-
singly frequent episodes of double vision on the part of the lens,
like an unresolved stereometric image. In those last fifteen
minutes, this double vision gradually takes hold, and for a minute
the third, bottom image — which remains unresolved long after
we can make out the 'walking woman' silhouettes — hovers
within another, larger, ghostly superimposed image of itself,
as if existing at two different focal distances at the same time,
as if the image had become a mirage. Finally, at about 41 minutes,
the bigger, closer version asserts itself — the zoom seems to jump

into it — and the photograph fills the entire screen. Only
at that point do we see the intricate web pattern and recognise
a black-and-white photograph of waves (fig.17). This revelation
is accompanied by the siren-like rise and fall of subsidiary sine
waves. Just as the sound of the sine wave rises into the register
of silence, the image goes out of focus, blurs and dissolves into
white (fig.18).

For most of the film, the camera does not itself move or advance,
but the zoom creates a sense that it is heading somewhere and
getting closer — even though the zoom only means a lens is
being turned, or that the visual field is narrowing. The effect is
a gradual compression of the space, as if it were being shovelled
against the far wall and displaced to the sides, in an unseen leak
at the edges of the screen. (Our eyes keep moving to the sides to
see if we can see the advance of the lens, as if we were watching
a shadow lengthen.) This flattening intensifies when the
initially oblique angle of the zoom changes to its final head-on
approach. Yet, in spite of this strange collapsed spatiality, we
also experience the zoom as our own virtual movement into depth
— not quite bodily, but through a feeling of being pulled forward
by our eyes, merely by looking. At the end, when the zoom closes
in on a smaller and smaller area of the waves, we feel that it
is actually carrying us into the photograph, in something like a
dream of flying, as if there were no barrier, as if the zoom could
puncture the photograph, wall and screen and move beyond them,
out into and over the waves.[13]

Another doubling of experience is created by the relationship
of the intensifying sine wave to the advancing zoom. Artists
were experimenting with sound and light environments in
New York at the time, to various 'psychoacoustical' effects.
From 1964, La Monte Young worked with sustained sine wave
drones, sometimes in combination with voices and instruments,

investigating the ways that fixed sounds tended to 'drift'.
(Snow describes the effect of harmonics 'banging together' above
the sounds, as if spatially precipitated out of them.)[14] Snow's
thinking about the sound for *Wavelength* began with the problem
of establishing a glissando that could continue for forty minutes
or so, and he considered using a trombone or violin; but a sine
wave generator proved more effective. The rise of *Wavelength*'s
single, glissando sine wave has a different effect from a drone:
over the course of the film, it moves from the low-end (50 cycles
per second) to the high-end inaudible (12,000), creating the
feeling of a linear acceleration that resonates with the seen
line of the zoom.[15] *Wavelength*, of course, is not a physical space
through and around which we can walk; but it capitalises on
the fact that we are watching and hearing from a fixed vantage
point: the reciprocal intensification of the mechanical lens and
rising sine make it seem as if the seen and the heard were being
converted into one another, with the slight shudders of the zoom,
caused by the imprecise fit of the different orders of sound and
light waves, apparently resisting that process.[16]

For example, in a brief passage just before 'Strawberry Fields
Forever' plays, the zoom hops backward slightly to recover ground
it has already covered; and again, after the event of the man's
death, an earlier shot is superimposed over the zoom's 'position',
giving the impression that it is pulling back from its own
inexorability. Yet as the zoom persists and pushes forward into
the space, we become vaguely aware of the interruptive shifts in
the zoom's focal length, which give it a speculative volition, as if
new decisions were continually being entertained. In effect, the
screen image seems to respond to the depicted events in the room,
creating the sense that the room is itself an organism responding
to entrances and intrusions, perhaps mimicking or cuing our
own responses: during 'Strawberry Fields Forever', for instance,
the image turns pinkish red, or during the startling sounds

before the man's entrance the image turns to a reddish grainy
fog, but shifts to clarity as he walks in. The sounds — glass
shattering, a kind of shoving and crunching as if walking on
broken glass — are outside the picture, and therefore experienced
as if in the off-screen space, our viewing space and then our
memory. A sustained passage of regular fluctuations of light
before the crashing noises creates an effect like shallow
breathing on the part of the image, suggesting that the film
or the room also have physiological responses to the 'suspense'
— and, indeed, this applies to the whole film, as its slow
directional movement creates an expectation that we are
being directed toward something, toward a definitive event.
The eruptions of different registers of light, colour and film
texture, the passages of intensely saturated red, green, mauve,
granular whiteness or reversal into negative, suggest movement
through different atmospheres or perceptual 'weather systems',
and create an intermittent buoyancy that alleviates the suspense
created by the protracted directional movement.[17]

Wavelength and 'Thots'

Wavelength was originally screened for a small circle of artists
and film-makers at the Filmmakers' Cinemathèque, and its
importance was immediately recognised.[18] Snow wrote his
first formal statement about *Wavelength* in 1967, when the
film was submitted to the fourth international experimental
film competition in Knokke-le-Zoute, Belgium, where it won
the grand prize. For all its sensuous accessibility, *Wavelength*
sent aerial roots into the intellectual culture of the time, from
the austerely structural and philosophical to the increasingly
theorised culture of popular mass media. The film, Snow said,
was meant to be a 'summation' of his 'nervous system, religious
inklings and aesthetic ideas' and 'thots', as they were in 1966.[19]
That same year, Susan Sontag had published a collection of essays,
Against Interpretation and Other Essays, in which she flagged the

'non-boundaries' of the vast new cultural landscape, and her
admiration for *nouvelle vague* films — as she said, films 'about
ideas' — set one stage for Snow's film about 'thots'.[20] Even while
she was apparently rejecting interpretation and 'meaning'
in favour of purely formalist responses to the sensuous surfaces
of things, the very scope and density of Sontag's intellectual
references installed erudition as a unique identifier of contemporary approaches to art, film and writing: when she called for
an 'erotics of art', she really proposed an erotics of cerebration.[21]
In 1965, the art critic Barbara Rose also set out the literary
and philosophical markers of a contemporary 'sensibility' for
artists. As for Sontag, many of these involved scepticism about
any 'meaning' under or beyond the surface of language or things,
and Rose too lists the usual intellectual suspects whose ideas can
be aligned with aspects of *Wavelength* — amongst them, Alain
Robbe-Grillet, Roland Barthes and Samuel Beckett.[22] Snow's film
delicately negotiates this erudition, perhaps playing on Rose's
observation that Minimalist objects had 'set the wave length
for art so low [that] it is finally inaudible'.[23]

The background of *Wavelength*'s accomplishment must include
Snow's having seen innumerable experimental films in New
York by film-makers such as Bruce Conner, Stan Brakhage,
Paul Sharits and Ernie Gehr. These film-makers experimented
with found footage, scratching and drawing into the material
surface of film, and creating strobing and flickering bombard-
ments that altered ordinary spatial and temporal perception.
Their repertoire — ironic, anomic or ecstatic — was endless.
Wavelength can be aligned with the tactic of unusually prolonged,
redundant or repetitive attention that effectively blurred the
boundaries between heightened acuity and absolute ignoring on
the part of the viewer. Snow's zoom could be seen to allude to the
very long duration of some of Andy Warhol's films, such as the
eight-hour shot of the Empire State Building in *Empire* (1964);

but, in contrast, *Wavelength* is a constructed — not a
'documentary realist' — recording, and the time of *Wavelength*
represents real time as well as taking place within it, as day
turns to night twice during its 45 minutes. (In Snow's DVD
WVLNT (*Wavelength for Those Who Don't Have the Time*) (2003),
Wavelength is projected in just 15 minutes as three superimposed
segments, creating an effect of rooms telescoped within the
room.) In fact, *Wavelength* might be seen as an alternative
to the ways Warhol taxed perceptual habits through sustained
shots of a single thing or through affectless, random zooming.[24]

Wavelength established itself as a beacon and touchstone of
intellectualism in film in Annette Michelson's foundational
essay, 'Toward Snow', published in the June 1971 issue of
Artforum. The magazine's cover image is a still from the film,
a view washed in mauve and blue, intensifying the yellow of
the chair. Snow exercised a redefining function for Michelson,
effected by his broad knowledge in the fields of art, music and
contemporary philosophy; crucially, his erudition necessitated
an erudite critic: 'most FILM critics now at work are simply
not nor ever will be equipped for the critical task on the
level which the present flowering of cinema in this country
demands'.[25] Accordingly, in September 1971, Michelson edited
a special film issue of *Artforum* as part of her project of bringing
artists' films out of the quarantine of film studies and film
journals, and of finding a vocabulary for the time-based work
that Michael Fried, the magazine's principal art critic at the
time, was not interested in addressing.[26] The stakes for the new
American independent film and its criticism in *Artforum* were
high: it had to stand up to radical cultural reassessments in
French journals such as *Critique* and *Tel Quel*, and, in the wake
of the strikes and protests in France in 1968, to theorising in
Cinéthique and *Cahiers du cinéma* about the ontology and political
function of film.

Wavelength navigates the intellectual premises of the art,
art-critical and film worlds of the late 1960s, registering these
in different tones — sceptical, witty, poetic and laconic — and
treating its extra-filmic concerns always so lightly that their
implications are firmly meshed with the experience of the
images and sounds. It is certainly possible to draw analogies
between it and the art and criticism of the time: the zoom could
be aligned with the line of bricks that make up Carl Andre's
Lever, exhibited in 'Primary Structures' (1966) at the Jewish
Museum in New York, or with La Monte Young's 'event' score,
Draw a Straight Line and Follow It (1961); the suffusing flushes
of filter colour might bring to mind Clement Greenberg's
mapping of flatness in colour field paintings, or Dan Flavin's
installations of coloured fluorescent light that seem to vaporise
the space they occupy.[27] Snow's own sculpture and painting is
another referent: for example, his sculpture *Shunt* (1959) snakes
down the wall and across the floor in a line that marks out
a prior concern with linear paths. Snow's comment that
Wavelength is 'in the air' may be a riposte to Fried writing in
Artforum that Jules Olitski dreamed of painting 'colours sprayed
in the air and remaining there'[28] — because, as Michelson would
later point out, film is inherently colours projected in the air.[29]
Snow consciously intended that the 'memory shape' of the zoom
should mirror the cone of the projector beam; and a feature of
Wavelength's shape has to do with the way that light is projected
from a small transparent still photograph and magnified to the
size of the screen, while the zoom's movement starts with the
'wide' shape on the screen but diminishes as it moves toward
a small still photograph.

It is hard not to imagine Snow having a bit of fun with
referencing his contemporaries. The yellow chair that faces us
for most of the film, for example, is both ordinary and auratic.
With the unassuming four-square pragmatism of a kitchen chair,

it grounds the three images above it and the approaching zoom —
but it is also a strangely shiny lure. As in George Brecht's Fluxus
Chair Events, which took place in New York in 1961, a chair,
itself inert, could become an environmental 'event' of the order
intimated in Snow's note 'all the events of one place'.[30] But his
chair could also be read in relation to Michael Fried's powerful
praise of Anthony Caro's yellow sculpture *Midday* (1960). Fried
had understood *Midday*'s subtle relations of parts to a whole
as being like a syntax, and therefore constituting a gesture that
intends to communicate, in contrast to Donald Judd's and Robert
Morris's Minimalist 'literalist' boxes and objects, which he
deplored. In this light, the chair's syntax of chromed legs and
rungs and yellow back (which Snow had in fact painted yellow
himself), could be taken as a kind of humble marker for *Midday*
as a heroically ordinary protagonist in art-world engagements.

At a time of expressed scepticism about meaning (reflected
in Susan Sontag's *Against Interpretation and Other Essays*),
the word Snow chose as the title of the film retained a fundamental allusiveness. As a disturbance whose pattern depends
on the properties of the medium it traverses, 'wavelength'
worked as a metaphor for a number of contemporaneous ideas,
which might include Modernist medium-specificity (since
film is made of wavelengths of light and sound), Marshall
McLuhan's world-as-radio, and Maurice Merleau-Ponty's
phenomenological account of the 'gesture' that marks our
immersive communication with the world, reformulated in
popular culture terminology as 'being on the same wavelength'.[31]
The notes Snow made in 1966 and 1967, arrayed as patterned
constellations of terms, were increa-singly structured as the
ambiguous binaries of Snow's next film <—> *Back and Forth*
(1968): 'disagreement — agreement / fight — fuck / reading —
dancing / game — questions (verbal) — answers (yes no head
shake) / <—> brush strokes / painting — erasing / windshield

wipers — alternating current' and 'write some dialogue — steal some'. Inside the word 'wavelength' a poetic oceanic comes up against a breakwater of structural, scientific rigour.[32]

Snow wrote in 1968 that he had wanted *Wavelength* to be a 'definitive statement'.[33] The simplicity of the film's structure has lent itself to being taken as a definitive statement of something, but in the service of different definitions: it has been described as 'axiomatic', 'structural', 'radical', 'epistemological' and 'formal'. It has been subject to critical claims and counterclaims.[34] Does *Wavelength* somehow constitute an ontology of film, or does it just raise the idea of ontology?[35] Does it restore a 'transcendent subject' with mastery over the perceptual field, both as author and as viewer, or does it block that suspect entity?[36] Does it somehow *enact* consciousness by provoking an intensified phenomenological experience in the viewer, or does it interfere with our sensory immersion by stimulating a disruptive undertow of self-awareness?[37] Is *Wavelength* reflexive, fulfilling the Modernist requirement that a work of art articulate its own medium? Or, is it a film *about* the Modernist requirement — made by both the Russian Formalism that influenced French literary thought at the time, and Clement Greenberg's and Michael Fried's writings about painting — that art should engage its own properties and devices?[38] It is, at one and the same time, about being conscious and about the consciousness of being conscious, about perceiving and being shown what perception is like: in it, the Modernist medium delineating itself is captured by the phenomenological ecstasy of bringing the world into being through our perception, in a kind of procedural auto-erotic asphyxiation.

How does one film lend itself to both being taken as a postmodern dispersal of the centred, authorial, empowered self, and as asserting authorial control? Could it equally serve a materialist, political reading? Manny Farber, writing in *Artforum*, almost immediately described the loft in *Wavelength* as a space 'in which a dozen businesses have lived and gone bankrupt'.[39] Nearly twenty years later, Yvonne Rainer inserted a clip from *Wavelength* into scenes of gentrifying New York loft renovations in her film *The Man Who Envied Women* (1986).[40] In Rainer's film, an excerpted passage of *Wavelength*'s intensely pulsating colours stands as a kind of lost Eden of affordable lofts where the 1960s community of New York artists lived and worked.

Materials are, of course, key: while Snow's Knokke-le-Zoute statement gives the impression of the film as an austere, aerated structure of abstracted equivalences and ideas, it was actually made as a complexly layered, handled, handmade, accretive physical project, in which film was marked, spliced and optically altered:

1. *I decided on the duration. The film was shot on 100-ft rolls of 16mm film, of various stocks. 100 ft is a little less than 3 minutes. It was going to use 16 to 18 rolls. I put a piece of white tape on the zoom lens. Opening shot to closing shot, I divided up the tape into 18 (?) equal sections then further subdivided that into tiny increments that I could follow as I turned the zoom lens by hand. I also divided up the film stocks into a selected numbered series of 1 to 18 (?)... I first shot the intruder falling to the floor. It was roll 10 or something but I knew where it was on the marked up zoom lens tape.*

2. *It was shot over a period of a few days, a week and a bit. Sometimes I would only shoot a single roll, other times for longer. The synch sound scenes were shot separately. I think the first 8 to 10 minutes (the book shelves delivery, etc.) were shot at the same time.*

3.	*I had to move the camera physically ahead for the last approximately 10 minutes.*

4.	*There were 2 or 3 alternate rolls from which I chose the 'best', otherwise it was splicing them all together. However, I was not completely satisfied with what had happened to the colour by my real-time use of the different film stocks and placing gels and plastics in front of the lens, so I made a 'B-roll' of colour changes which are supered here and there in the film. The effect is quite different from the in-front-of-the-lens gels. Also there are on the same B-roll, the super-imposition of the phone call, frames of the opening shot placed later in the film and the super-imposition of the final moves onto the wave photo. There are other super-impositions done in editing where I placed the zoom 'ahead' against the zoom 'behind' with the two eventually 'catching up'. That is what was done at the end where the further forward wave photo is supered for a time over the further back photo with a 'coming' to the final framing. Climax, that's what I thought.*[41]

Wavelength clearly relied on both a foreseen system (the tape and markings on the lens to establish the positions of the manual zoom, and the planned splicing from different rolls of film), and on the element of the unforeseen inherent in experimentation (including the use of outdoor film indoors under fluorescent or incandescent light, of outdated film stock, of changes in exposure). Saying that *Wavelength* was 'shot with a fixed camera from one end of an 80-foot loft, shooting the other end, a row of windows and the street' — as Snow did in his statement for Knokke-le-Zoute — streamlines the account. While that description matches the final product, it is also true that Snow started filming the zoom in the middle, with the man's death (but, to be clear about any putative symbolism, this was just because it was convenient for film-maker Hollis Frampton,

a friend of Snow's and the actor who played the dying man,
to do the scene that day). It is also noteworthy that the approach
to the wave photograph at the end of the film lay *beyond* the
reach of the zoom, and therefore the camera had to be physically
moved forward for the last ten minutes or so. The final approach
to the wave photograph is more directly head-on and, with
the superimposition of the wave photograph, slightly stalling
— as if somehow the screen were holding out against the lens
before pushing through and jumping into the wave photograph.
By being extended in this effectively makeshift way, the
zoom becomes a metaphor for Marshall McLuhan's aphorism:
'Man's reach must exceed his grasp or what's a metaphor?'[42]

The stakes for the line of the zoom were extremely high, and,
because of its simplicity, it became a hanger for the ideas shaping
Wavelength — as well as for the subsequent shaping of the idea
of structuralism in film. It could stake out Jorge Luis Borges's
recently translated parable of the mythic labyrinth, reconfigured
here as a 'single line, invisible and unceasing'.[43] This relies
on a philosophical parable, Zeno's paradox of motion, which is
explained by the example of an arrow in flight: a moving arrow
is necessarily immobile at each moment, always stuck at some
midpoint between two points in its trajectory. This notion
of time as both fluid and stopped and of space as both expansive
and divisible into impossibly narrow slots inflects all film,
as film is the movement of still images. Snow's zoom could
work as an allegory of apperception, the process by which the
mind brings experiences and memories to bear on our senses,
unifying the flow of sensation, or of film itself as a succession
of stills in which the perceptible adjustments of the lens stand
for the imperceptible modification of successive film frames.[44]
The zoom is a kind of scale marking our experience of time as one
of both loss and accumulation. Like Zeno's arrow, *Wavelength*'s
zoom can work as a metaphor for any number of things:

perceptual processes, chronological measurement, directional movement, line of sight, teleological history or narrative of any kind. At the time of its making and ever since, *Wavelength* has functioned as an allegorical structure *par excellence*, situated within any number of scientific, philosophical, sociological and popular cultural narratives. In 1967 Snow wrote that *Wavelength* had originated as a summation of 'everything that I've thought about, everything', but wryly concluded that in fact 'it doesn't really mean anything' — that is, it does not mean any *one* thing.[45]

McLuhan, Leary and the Popular Culture of Consciousness

If, as Snow has also said, *Wavelength* is 'metaphysics', it is a strange metaphysics, in the sense that the phenomenological idea of immersive embodied perception of time and space is its driving abstract force.[46] Snow's notes reveal his interest in phenomenology, realised in his sculptures *Blind* and *Scope* (both 1967), which were meant to be seen *through*, construing the structure of the artwork as a form of heightened perception, 'a director of attention' that somehow 'instructs' the spectator's 'identification', channelling and framing 'concentration' and focusing vision.[47] In 1966, though, philosophical pheno-menology was filtered in the US through the thinking of a pervasive public intellectual, Marshall McLuhan. In McLuhan's view, the technological shift from a print-based world to the encompassing, audio-visual environment of radio, television and other electronic media had provoked a cultural crisis and the numbing of the collective sensorium.[48] He envisioned the artist's task as establishing new perceptual modes by creating works that could adjust the spectator's senses, numbed by over-load, to the synaesthetic barrage of new electronic media. There is a McLuhanist touch in *Wavelength*, when the women listen to 'Strawberry Fields Forever' on the radio rather than a record player; part of the importance of this for Snow is that a radio is

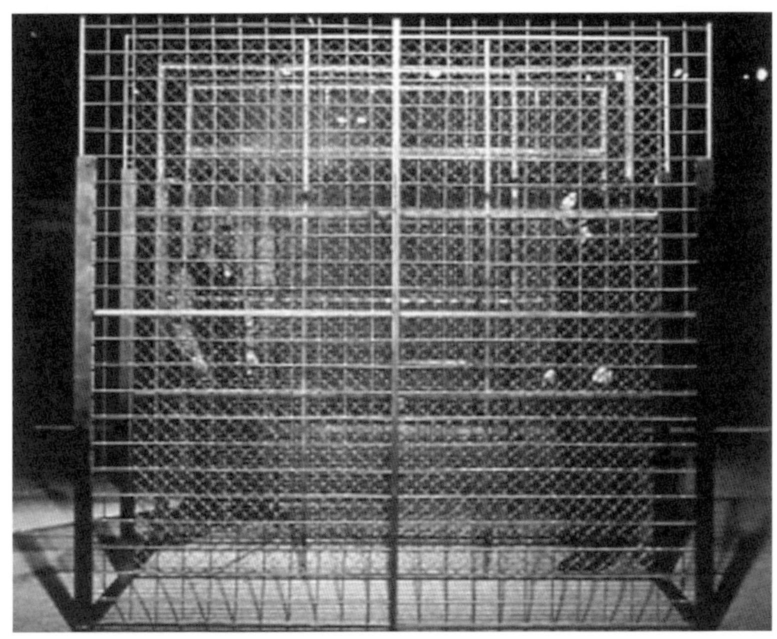

Michael Snow,
Blind, 1967,
painted aluminium and steel,
243.8 × 243.8 × 243.8cm
National Gallery of Canada,
Ottawa

sound coming in from outside — an aural window. (Later, the telephone is sound that goes *out* of the room.) For McLuhan, radio was the new 'tribal horns and antique drums', linking electronic modes of perception to ancient forms, bringing the psyche and society into a 'single echo chamber'.[49] Snow's particular choice of The Beatles hit of early 1967 is interesting, in that the song brokered a new technology, the Melotron, an ancestor of the synthesiser. The song's distinctive warping sound, produced by melding two separate taped versions that had been recorded at different speeds, enhances the feeling of something slightly alien. Snow actually post-synced 'Strawberry Fields Forever' into *Wavelength*, since he found what was actually playing on the radio during filming — Joan Baez's Christmas hit of 1966, 'The Little Drummer Boy' — intolerable, and it is not hard to imagine how absurd the 'rum pum pum pum' chorus would sound with the sine wave. (This is the one instance when Snow abandoned his prior decision to accept whatever sounds happened to occur during the filming.) When he declared *Wavelength* a 'summation' of his 'nervous system',[50] it was in a McLuhanist spirit: 'with electricity we extend our central nervous system globally'.[51] In 1968, when Joyce Wieland, at the time married to Snow, invited McLuhan to a screening of *Wavelength*, she promised him 'total sound saturation', presumably because it seemed like the kind of new acoustic space McLuhan would like. His secretary declined on his behalf, however, because surgery had left the theorist with an aggravated sensitivity to noise.[52]

McLuhan, in turn, was filtered through the LSD culture that had become mainstream by 1966. In September of that year, *LIFE* magazine described the emergent type of the 'psychedelic' artist in McLuhanist terms as mediating the new collective electronic consciousness with new media such as strobe lights, distorting goggles, rapidly changing slides and a prolonged 'nerve-wracking drone', to simulate the perceptual effects of drugs.[53] The cover of

a special 'LSD issue' of March 1966 was a black-and-white
photograph of a hand holding gels printed in colour, suggesting
literal filters of perception. Snow did hold filters in front
of the lens in filming *Wavelength,* and reused those filters in
Untitled Slidelength (1969—71), in which plastic transparencies
act as perceptual intensifiers.[54] By 1966 the phenomenological
image of human experience as a 'motivated' journey was a 'trip'
and the sine wave an 'om'.[55]

Snow associated *Wavelength* with acid, writing that 'films are
like drugs which teach', forming 'states of consciousness' in the
'mind space' of the spectator.[56] His expressed 'religious inklings'
in the film could be aligned with the acid guru Timothy Leary's
crypto-mystical visions of the 'trip', reverberating in *Wavelength*
as lights, music and colours that dissolve into 'latticeworks of
pulsating white waves', preceding the sense of being alone in
a 'dead impersonal world'.[57] What we might call the slow
strobing of *Wavelength* — flashing that never quite boots up to
strobe speed in spite of our sense that it might — aligns with
Jonas Mekas's account of the acid experience in the winter 1966
'Expanded Arts' issue of *Film Culture,* especially of the way that
strobing fragments the world in a weird 'temporal aliasing'
that approximates a mystical experience, both liberating and
deathly.[58] The trance-like aspect of *Wavelength* also seems to
acknowledge film's controversial capacity for inducing passivity
in the viewer with its play of light, shadow and colour, which
Christian Metz explored a decade later in *Le Signifiant imaginaire:
Psychanalyse et cinéma* (1977).[59] In 1963, the film theorist
Jean Mitry, in *Esthétique et psychologie du cinéma,* described the
film goer as suspended between dream and daydream, liable to
wishful projection (and, therefore, in need of resuscitation by
critique).[60] *Wavelength* goes with, rather than against, that flow:
Snow seems to have entertained the idea of using as part of the
soundtrack Billy Strayhorn's 1940 jazz recording 'Day Dream'

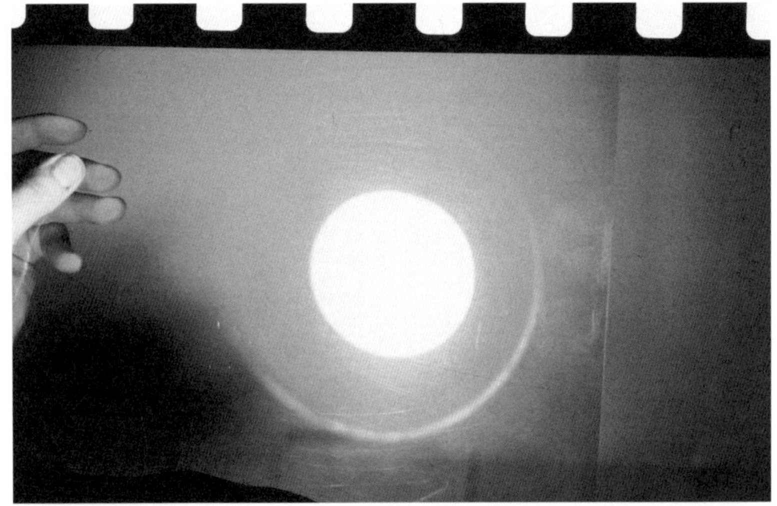

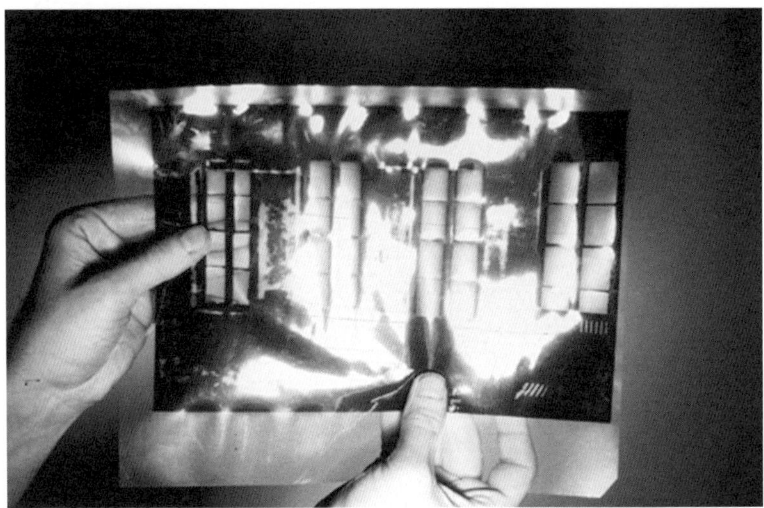

Michael Snow,
Untitled Slidelength, 1969—71,
eighty 35mm colour slides
National Gallery of Canada, Ottawa

(whose lyric 'everything seems unreal now' echoes 'nothing is real' from 'Strawberry Fields Forever').[61]

If Leary's account of the characteristic acid 'distension of time' played through new film-making, it also reinforced literary and art-critical interest in 'distension', a key concept in the Russian Formalist analysis of narrative that was at the time being translated in France and expanding into broader critical discourse.[62] Distension was a technique for making texts difficult in various ways, by means of extending their length or intensifying the experience of their length in order to demand more of the reader and to avoid what were considered shallower gratifications, such as accessible content, narrative pull or reality effect. Michelson variously used distension to describe the temporal art of John Cage, Robert Morris and Snow.[63] It certainly seems to be a way to identify one of the things that Snow was getting at: one of his notes reads 'buy "You keep me hangin' on"?', referring to the November 1966 hit by The Supremes — though the song would have probably been too obvious a commentary.[64]

Time and Space
In his Knokke-le-Zoute statement Snow restaged the classical unities of time, space and action as the 'cosmic equivalents of setting, action, zoom and room'; in doing so, he signalled by echo location his own position within dominant moves and discourses. It has been argued that the 1960s marked a spatial turn in Western culture, in both science and in art, in which space — physical, mental, natural, social, imaginary — was no longer thought of as an inert container for historical operations nor as a dead ground for the passage of time.[65] It has equally been argued that this decade marked a *temporal* turn under the warping sway of new technology.[66] Plotting time and space (from Leibniz to Einstein) in terms of one another can mean

a relative perceptual weighting — does our most authentic
or legitimate experience reside mainly in time or in space,
and in what proportion? It could also mean plotting the relative
ideological perniciousness of one or the other. The zoom can be
taken in two ways: as either coring out the territorial power
of space by invasive temporal turns of the lens, or as spatial
interruptions of time conceived as linear inexorability.[67] When
Snow wrote that the 'structuring of time and the duration of
things interest me as well as the realisation of total time-shapes
that have a beginning and end', his term 'time-shapes' draws
Wavelength into the gravitational field of time as it was being
recalibrated in philosophy, history, narrative theory, popular
science, technology and systems theory.[68] It certainly acknowledges George Kubler's *The Shape of Time* (1962), an ambient text
in the New York art world during the 1960s that retrieved the
different registers of time in any given artefact.[69] The Annales
historian Fernand Braudel's vast conception of *'longue durée'*
— the infinitely slow timescale that converts into geography
and geology — could be used to reinforce the fashionable literary
interest in prolongation, duration and boredom as perceptual
intensifiers, and could apply specifically to zoom and sine wave
in *Wavelength*, against the relatively inconsequential *'histoire
événementielle'* of Snow's '4 human events'.[70] What, then, might
be the times — literary, theological, historical and so on —
of *Wavelength*?

There is, first of all, time as it was constituted in the narrative
texts and theatre of those years. More generally, we can hear
echoes of the time of Samuel Beckett's *Waiting for Godot* (1952) or
Endgame (1957) in Snow's writing: 'There won't be any summing
up. Perhaps there will', 'Is this the end? ... It's very close.'[71]
Beckett's theatre of doldrums forms around waiting for something that never happens, thereby staging eternity in real time.
Snow says of *Wavelength* that 'from the beginning the end is a

factor ... not "arbitrary", but fated', situating this fate in the
inevitability of something that is recorded. His remarks echo
something Robbe-Grillet noted about Beckett's work: in it,
he wrote, an 'ineluctable "here"' confronts an 'eternal "now"',
shutting down all notions of temporal progress and direction
except for the threat of the future as death — 'at once terrible
and fated'.[72] While there could be this narrative eschatology at
work in *Wavelength*, there is some complexity to its 'fated' end.

The idea that the end was present in the beginning of the film
was almost immediately recognised and taken exception to.[73]
Simon Hartog wrote that 'the film finishes when it starts,
because the end is included in its single frame'.[74] Conversely,
Steve Reich wrote to Snow right after seeing the film, pointing
out the uncertainty about the zoom's final destination for much
of the film.[75] Michelson, too, argued that at the beginning of
the film we do *not* know where it will end up.[76] These reactions
could be understood through the systems theory of the time,
the study of the mechanisms of any and all systems, thought
to be fundamentally the same whether in social organisations
or sciences.[77] With respect to *Wavelength*, two aspects of systems
theory particularly pertain: the notion of an open system and
the operation of feedback. When Michelson argued that we
cannot predict the zoom's destination at the start, she is heading
off any attribution of a teleological or theological movement
toward a predestined end. The efflorescence of the systems theory
concept of 'feedback', in which the past performance of a system
is fed back into the system in order to predict and modify its
future performance, was pervasive in the 1960s engagement with
time, and it offered a secular metaphor for predestination and
prophecy.[78] It was adapted by McLuhan to describe the end of
linear models of history and time in an image of the world folded
back on itself, in which nature finally becomes 'artefactual',
cybernetic, a work of art.[79] We can see the situation toward the

end of *Wavelength*, when the photograph of the waves hovers
within a larger superimposed version of itself that fills the
frame, as nature becoming artefact, folding back on itself.
There is also a minor enigma in the beginning of *Wavelength*:
when the shelves are brought in we notice that there is an
unpainted patch of wall marking the exact space where they
are to be placed, making it clear that they had probably occupied
that same space before being removed for the film in order to be
brought in again. Snow's attention to 'prophecy and memory' in
the Knokke-le-Zoute statement taps into recursive temporalities.

Wavelength's incremental adjustments of the lens also open
into the paradoxes of time-space in the quantum physics of
the 1960s: is each moment defined by new lines of time or space,
into parallel worlds? In the film, each turn of the lens seems
both decisive and optional, as if marking not only its own
moment, imposed by Snow's turn of the wrist, but also by the
turn not taken. Snow's zoom is a kind of test drive of human
experience, opening to the cool fact that each choice both implies
and eliminates alternatives. In *Wavelength*, the range of events
that lie outside the human incidents (including the little jumps
caused by splices, adjustments to focal length, shifts between
film stock, interposed flares of light and passages of solid colour)
are immediately grasped as gestures communicating choice,
made against whatever philosophical or theoretical ground and,
at the same time, materially independent of theory or precedent
— at least relatively so.

The temporality of *Wavelength* is also meted out by the series of
'4 human events'. They are enigmatic, and seem at the very least
to raise the question of why they are there. The empty shelves
being moved in make us think that something will happen
involving the shelves — that they might be filled — but nothing
does. Yet these heavy objects, we eventually realise, have passed

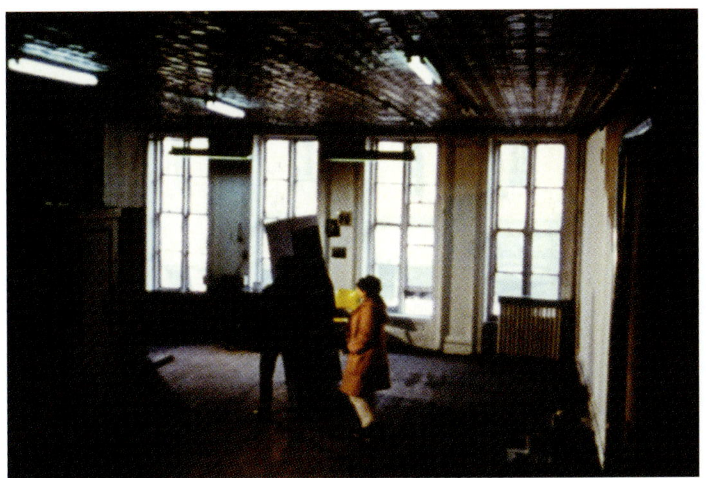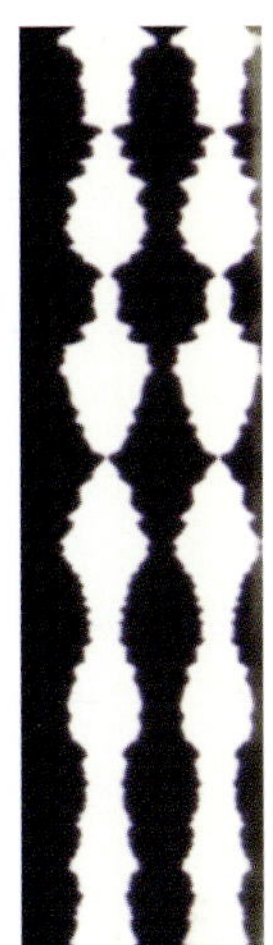

1—18. Michael Snow,
Wavelength, 1966—67,
16mm colour film,
45min, stills

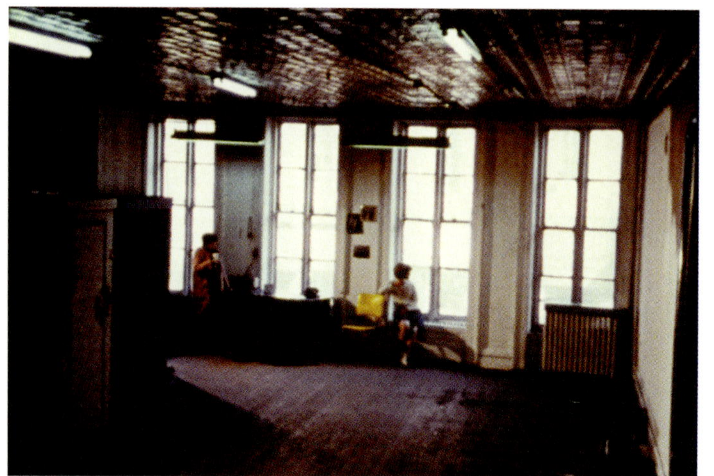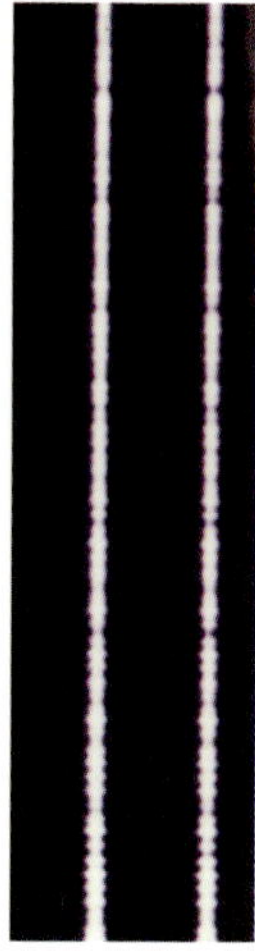

2.

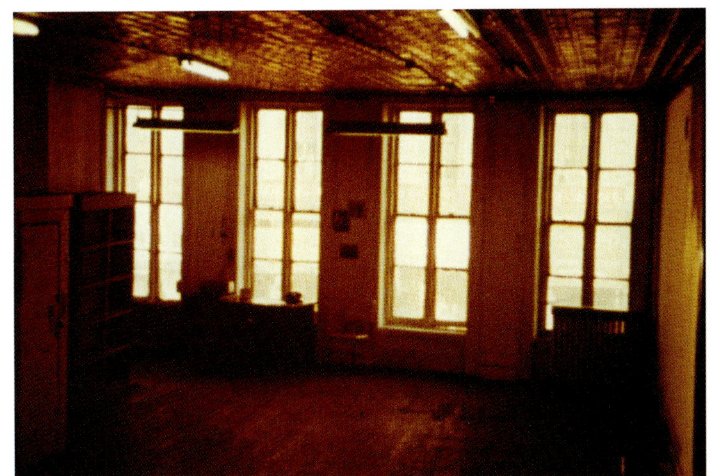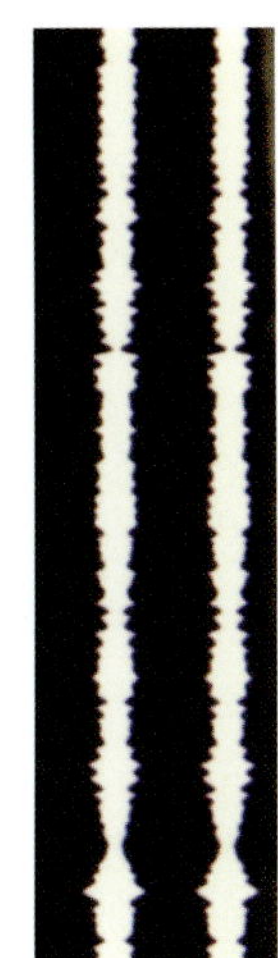

3.

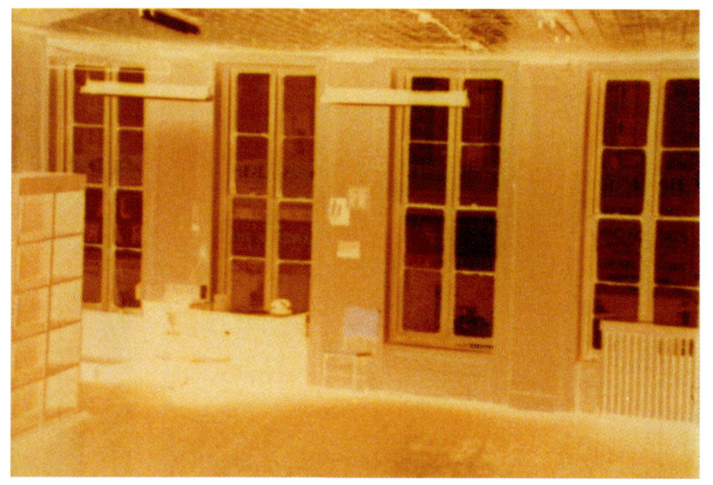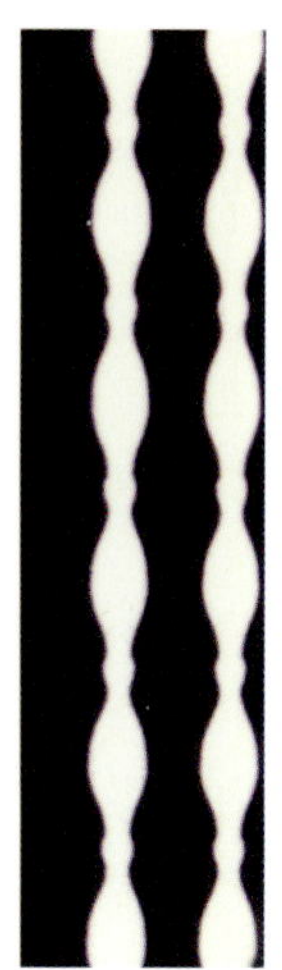

4.

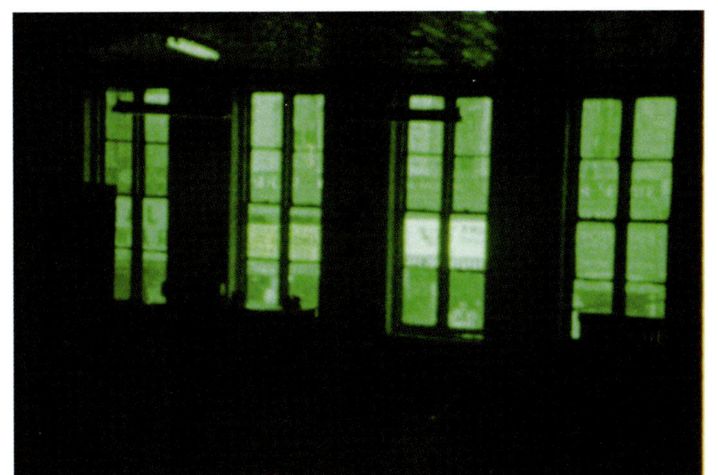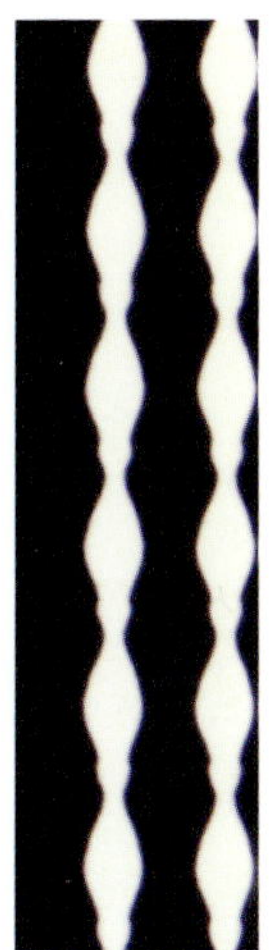

5.

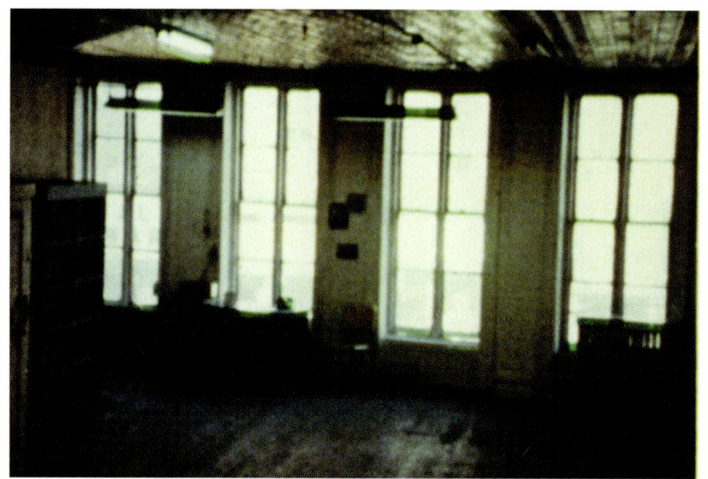 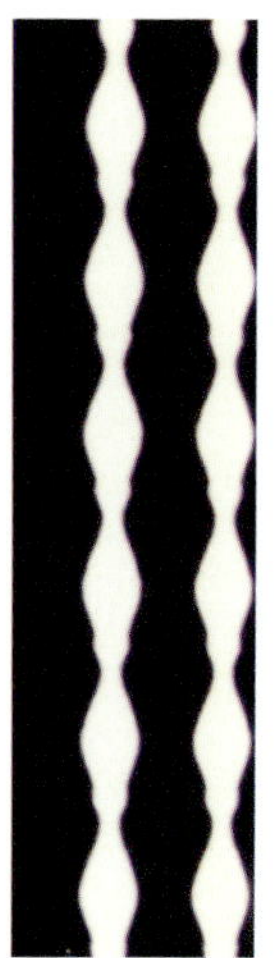

6.

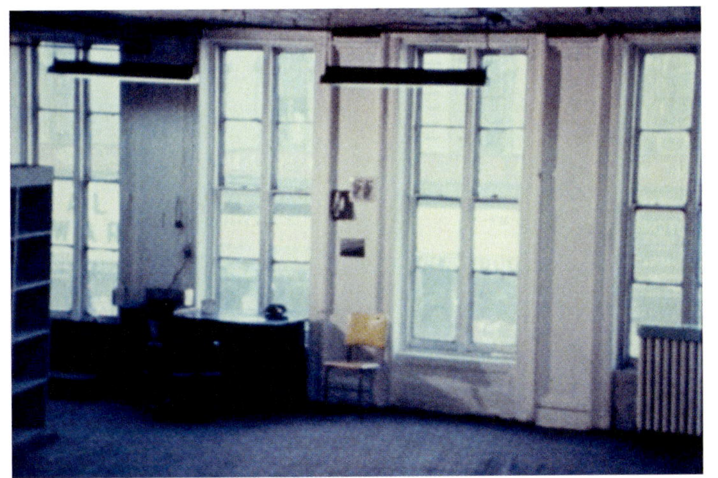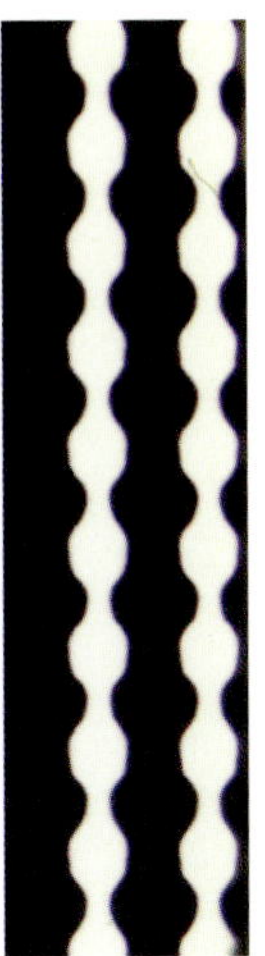

7.

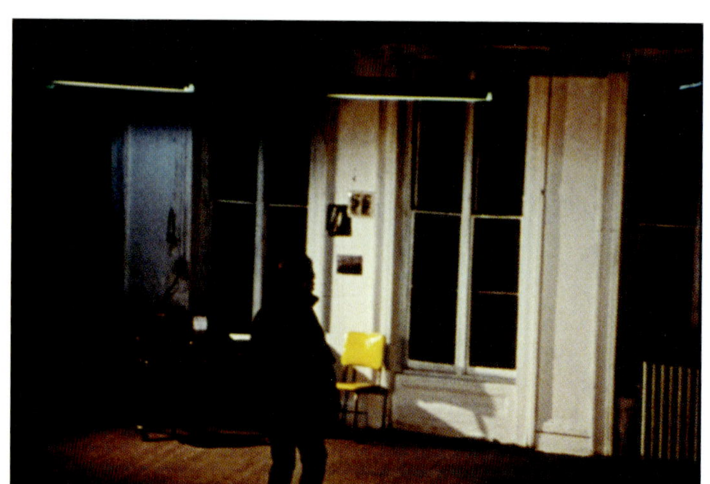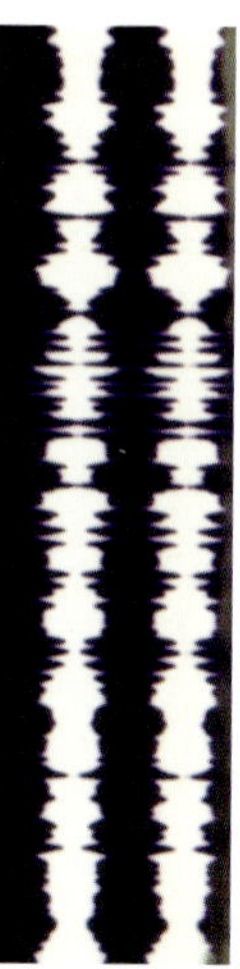

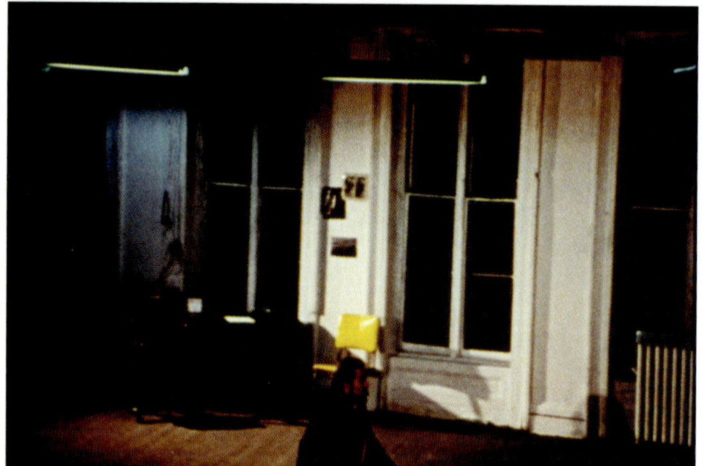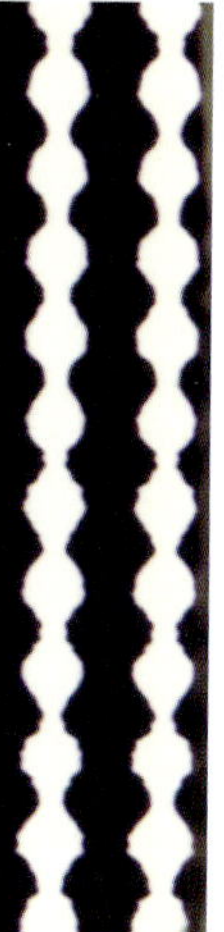

8—9.

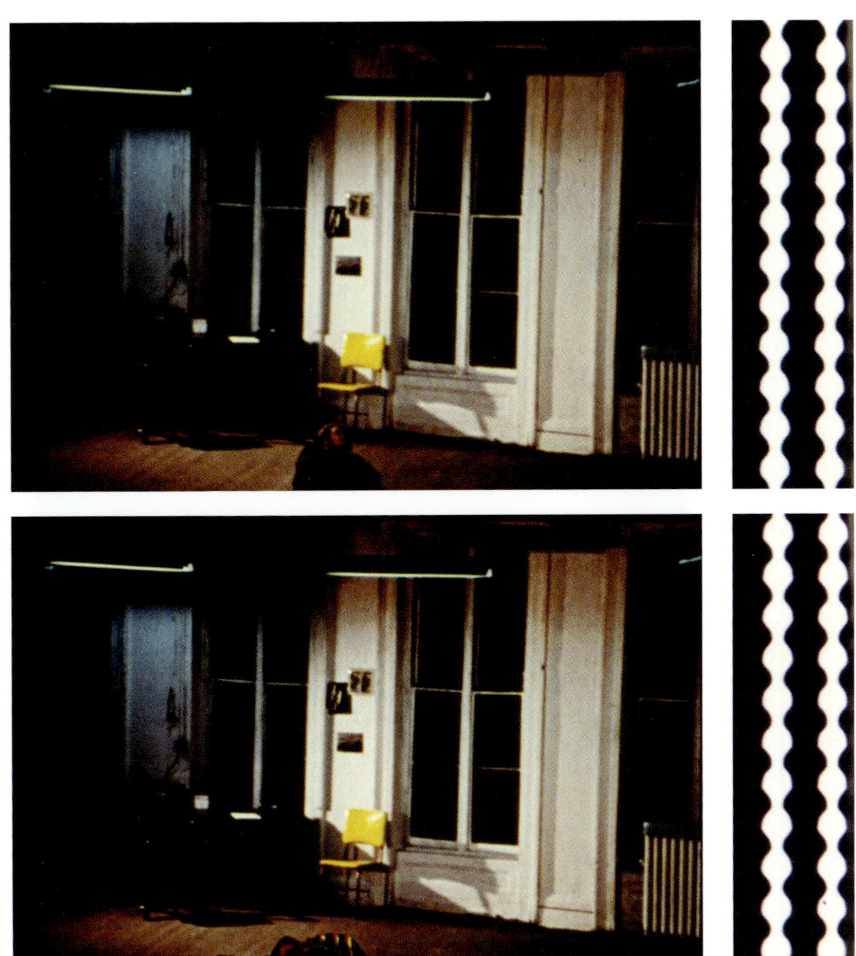

10—11.

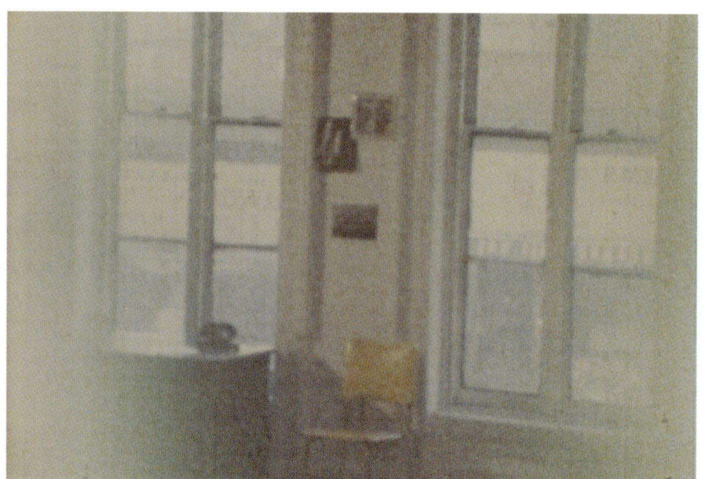

12.

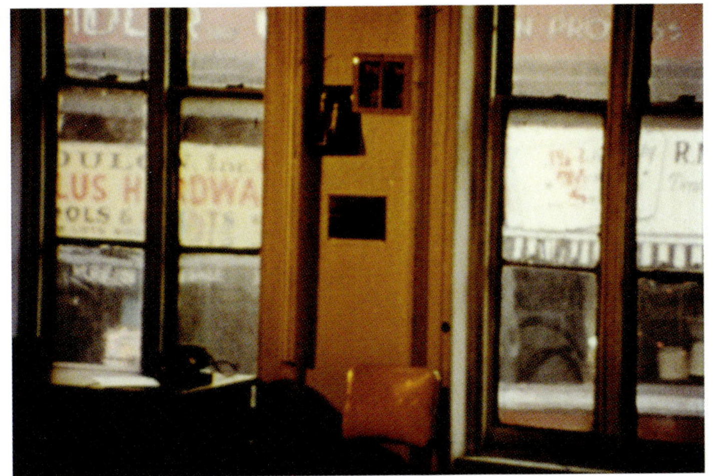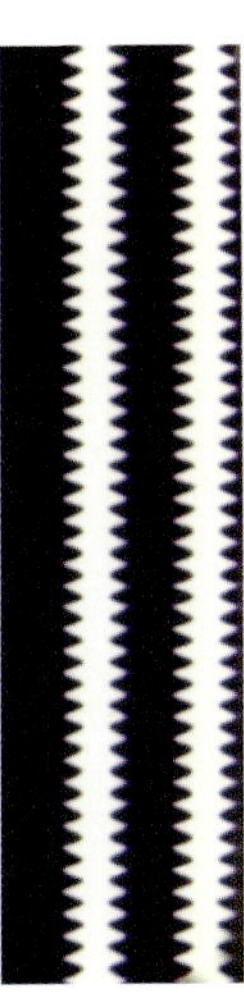

13.

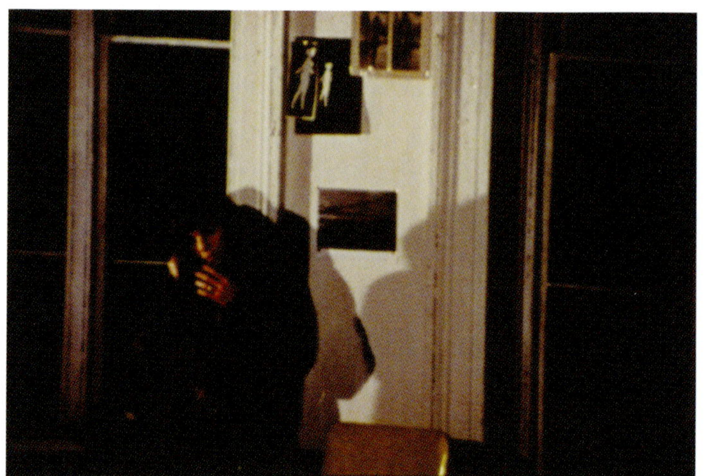

14.

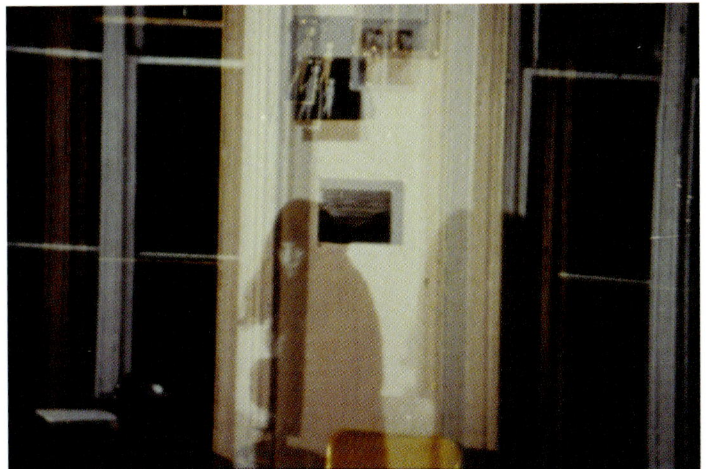

15.

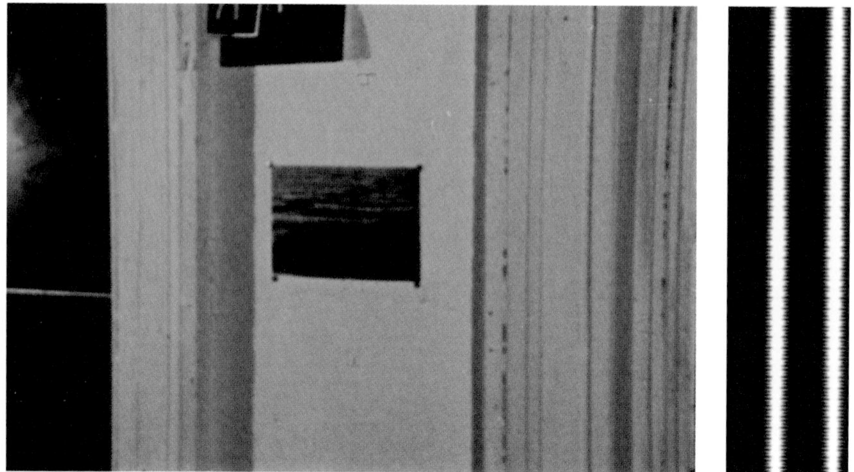

16.

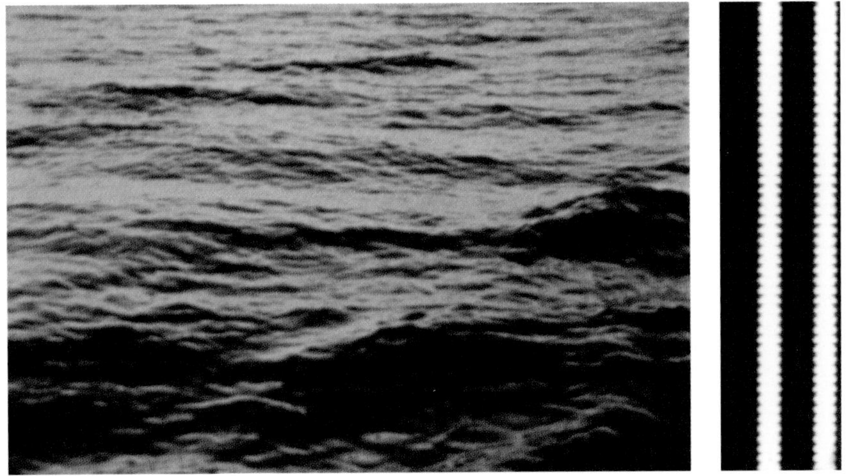

17.

18.

into our memory. It is hard to imagine a situation in which the women would briskly enter the loft, sit and drink coffee, listen to the radio and then abruptly leave, without conversation — unless they, too, were waiting for something that doesn't happen. The extended noise of breaking glass that precedes the man's entry reinforces the apparently inexorable course of the zoom and builds tension, but the actual event of his death is almost comically notional, as if an actor were practising how to hit a mark. Snow says that death installs the man in the realm of objects, and he is, like the shelves, moved to the domain of our memory. That memory is referred to by the fourth human event: the young woman calling to report finding the body, played by the actor and art critic Amy Taubin in a scene comparatively realistic and compelling — that is, more like a scene from a movie — and with an intensity completely at odds with the other events. Though Snow retrospectively said that he had no interest in narrative and no interest in subverting it, the incidents in *Wavelength* can be taken as being *about* narrative, or *about* structuralist accounts of narrative.[80] Conventional narrative, as a causal sequence of events, had been discredited as being complicit in the creation of critically debilitating illusion. *Wavelength* may be seen as, for example, a covertly humanistic version of Robbe-Grillet's aloof, obsessively redun-dant descriptions of objects and scenes, which were meant as paradoxical evidence of the psychopathy of humanising them.[81]

Snow's '4 human events' could also be textbook cases of what Roland Barthes has called '*actants*', events which prolong or exacerbate narrative as suspense. In his 'Introduction to the Structural Analysis of Narratives' (1966), Barthes lists events from a James Bond movie: having a drink, putting down a cigarette, making a phone call. Apparently insignificant, these are *actant* behaviours, which have nothing really to do with character or verisimilitude.[82] We find a list of similarly

structural 'movie actions' jotted down by Snow in his notes:
reading, applying makeup, dressing up, putting on a record, doing
exercises, opening and closing a window and making a telephone
call (though another action that Snow contemplated in his
notes for the film, 'masturbating', seems to be more of a parody
of a structural device to prolong narrative).[83]

The zoom across the loft is also omnivorous with respect to
the physics, philosophy and poetics of twentieth-century
space. Snow's phrases — 'beauty and sadness of equivalence',
the 'cosmic equivalence' of events, room and zoom — echo the
terms of Sigfried Giedion's magisterial history, *Space, Time
and Architecture* (1941), in which the artist provides what
he calls 'equivalents' — that is, humanising qualities such
as feeling, intuition and imagination that might soften the
shattering physics and technologies of the twentieth century.[84]
In calling for new ways of articulating space as not just
something seen but as a tactile, expansive experience involving
all the senses and bodily movement, McLuhan took up the
phenomenological understanding of space described by
Merleau-Ponty as a palpable 'field of presence in space and
time'.[85] New spatial environments, understood through all
the senses, could supersede the constricting, diagrammatic
visual organisation of the system of vanishing-point
perspective.[86] The narrowing zoom and rising sine wave in
Wavelength can be felt as compressing and intensifying, in an
analogue to seeing as a movement into the *depths* of 'visibility'
— as if seeing were analogous to entering space as a liquid
pressurised medium.

At the same time, the raking floorboards and receding lines
of the ceiling, fluorescent tubes and shelves collectively seem
to offer a vestigial cone of deep vanishing-point perspective
that sets the course of the zoom. Perspectival schemata imply

a human seeing 'subject' standing outside and in front of a perspectivally organised picture or proscenium stage, for whom an ideally coherent visual world is being unfurled. By 1966, this subject had already been picked apart in film theory. Did Snow, who said he had raised the camera in *Wavelength* in order to have a clearer view out the windows, inadvertently create a more 'lyric God-like above-it-all feeling', designing a set-up that capitulates with a kind of flattering of the viewing subject?[87] The actual situation in *Wavelength* seems more persuasively unstable. At the time, perspective was a bugbear of big minds: Michael Fried dismissed Tony Smith's euphoric account of a joyride on the unfinished New Jersey Turnpike, enhanced by the 'approach or onrush' of perspective, as a kind of perceptual cheap thrill.[88] If, as Snow argued, *Wavelength* had 'no perspectival space', then his point was surely made in the context of McLuhan's premise that the *content* of every new medium is the *form* of a prior medium.[89] That is, the floorboards of the loft may seem to mark out a perspective-like linear recession into depth, but they are only a reference to perspective as content or subject matter, not as a structuring system, since the zoom compresses and flattens as it goes. Put into McLuhan's terms, perspective in *Wavelength* would be a cliché used as a 'probe' (Snow noted 'room probe') into the hidden environmental structures of culture.[90] In the film, the apparent mastery implied by a fixed, raised vantage point is played against a cool exclusion, as the scene always seems to slip from our sight before it comes fully into focus — or, to use George Kubler's words, 'the moment of actuality slips too fast by the slow, coarse net of our senses'.[91] The passages of intense colour and flashing light make us feel that the world is being transmuted into new substances — with light itself giving up its ordinary role of making other things visible while being invisible, and instead shaking apart into its component spectral colours, taking on mote-like textures, turning into a particle accelerator and prism. But even if this is the case, these fascinating visual effects are pared away by the narrowing field of the zoom.

The final problem of a perspectival set-up is the question of exactly what happens at the vanishing point. Through much of *Wavelength* we are aware of the space beyond the windows, and it seems at the beginning that if the zoom were headed towards a specific place, it would be out of a window — in fact, early in the film a small window is open. But as the zoom advances, the windowpanes become flat, black obstacles, as impenetrable as the pictures on the wall. Robert Rauschenberg had written about the peculiar effects of windows: 'A dirty or foggy window makes what is outside appear to be projected onto the window plane', and images of shop signs seen through a window can become part of the flat collage of images on a wall.[92] These words might describe the situation in *Wavelength*, too, when 'all becomes surface' — photograph, painting, dirty windows and reflections. In 1967, Robert Smithson also wrote about the way that the traditional painting-as-window metaphor ought to be turned to the contentless surface and grid: 'A wall is in effect an opaque window.'[93] Here Smithson engages, intentionally or not, with the implications of a passage in the night sequence in *Wavelength* in which a smeared doodle shows up on the opaque black window like a finger-painting.

The exchange of transparency and opacity between window and wall finally takes the form of the zoom's not going out of a window after all; instead, there is a sudden moment when the viewer notices that the new 'centre' of the screen is the photograph of waves. As the waves fill the frame, the progress of the narrowing zoom gives the impression of moving *into* the image, out over the waves. This movement is something like the conceit of a punctured canvas — as in Lucio Fontana's slashed white canvases, which won the Grand Prize for painting at the

1966 Venice Biennale, or Niki de Saint Phalle's bullet holes
(1961—64), in which an actual tear annihilates the vanishing
point as the repository of discredited illusionism. These works
literalise the notion of the creative 'breakthrough' or 'destructive
liberation' that unleashes expression.[94]

At the very least, the vanishing point is where things stop.
Snow's use of perspective not only comments on perspective
itself, but also suggests an allegory in which pictorial perspective — the representation of spatial depth as converging lines
— is symbolically attached to the phenomenological act
described as a journey toward a horizon: 'there is a kind
of essence of death always on the horizon of ... thinking,' wrote
Merleau-Ponty.[95] Hollis Frampton similarly described the
movement toward death as being 'toward a vanishing-point
in rectilinear space'.[96] Early perspectival schemata seem to have
a deathly tendency, with bodies laid out as if succumbing to the
fatal power of the receding lines. In one famous example, Paolo
Uccello's *Niccolò Mauruzi da Tolentino at the Battle of San Romano*
(1438—40), a soldier lies dead on the orthogonal. Snow has said
that from the outset he wanted to have a body on the floor and to
'have the camera pass over it' in order to dramatise the inexorability of the zoom's passage. So in the film, the dying man falls,
feet toward the camera, right in the line of the zoom.[97]

The implications of perspective and vanishing point took on
particular weight in psychoanalytic film theory in the early
1970s, and eventually presented other ways of seeing *Wavelength*.
In the decade following its making, the film's peculiar staging
of the long zoom (long in length at 24 metres, and long in
duration at 45 minutes) could be seen in terms of Jacques Lacan's
construction of the 'gaze' in *The Four Fundamental Concepts of
Psychoanalysis* (1966) as a force field that ricochets the vanishing
point back onto the viewing subject, making the viewer its

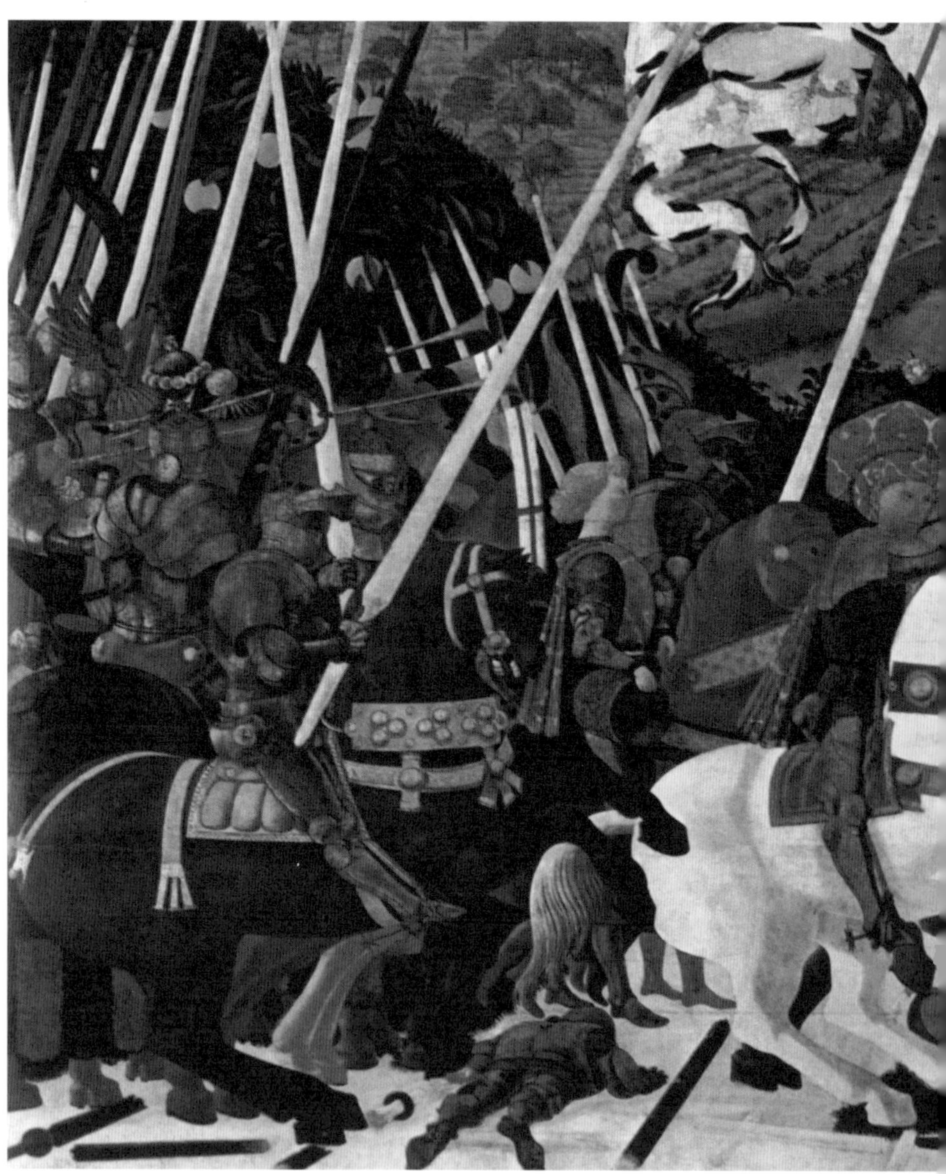

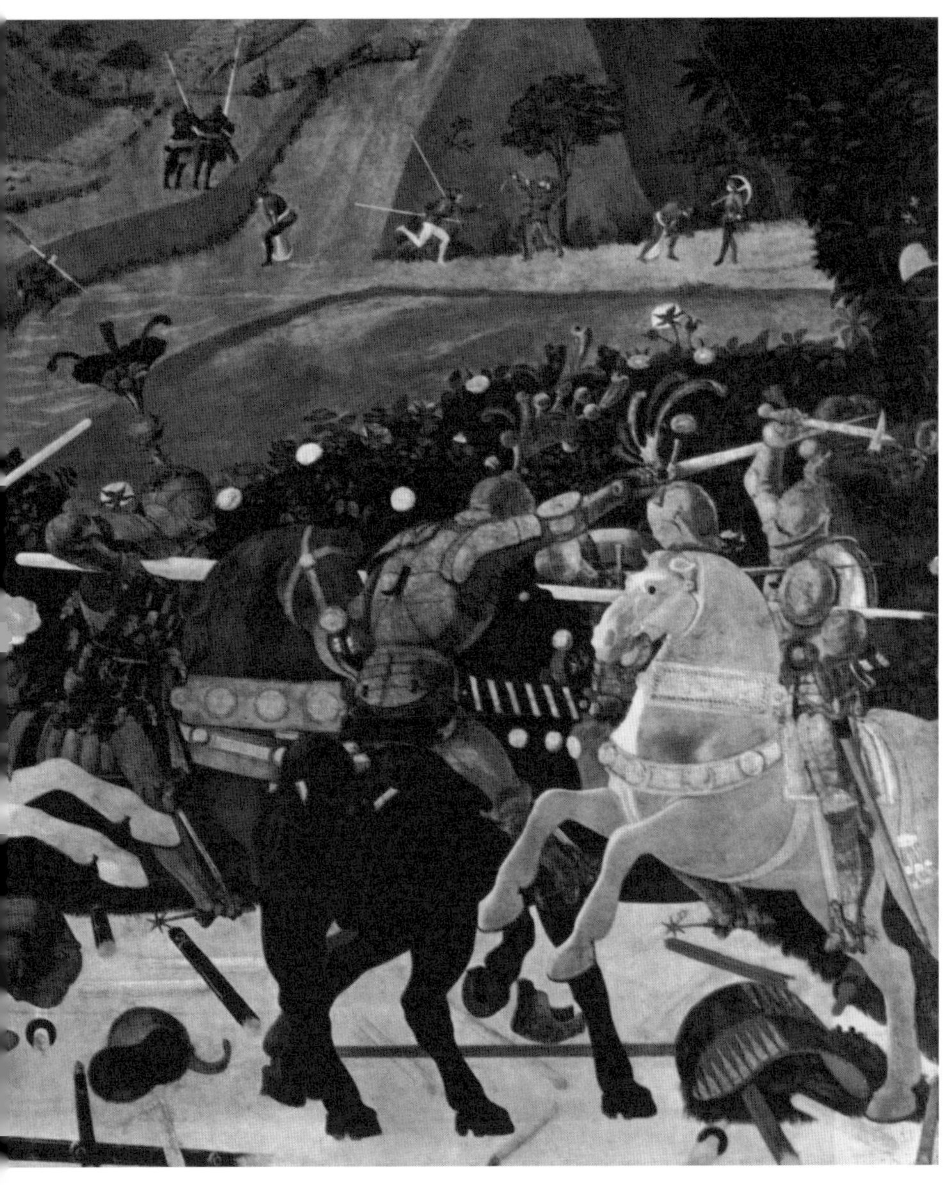

Paolo Uccello,
Niccolò Mauruzi da Tolentino at the Battle of San Romano, 1438—40,
egg tempera with walnut and linseed oil on poplar, 182 × 320cm
National Gallery, London

'punctiform object', or, more tellingly, its 'point of vanishing being'.[98] Perspective serves this annihilating analysis: Lacan conceives it as a web of lines mapping deep space on a flat plane — as if light were a thread joining point to point, forming a snare in which the subject is 'caught, manipulated, captured in the field of vision'.[99] Subsequently, key theorists of cinema, including Jean-Louis Baudry and Christian Metz, worked in the glare of Lacan's gaze, setting forth a scenario in which the film goer is a passive focal subject, complicit with the film's illusions of perspective and immobilised by the screen's Medusa-like image.[100] This version of the hyper-complicit viewer takes us to the place of *Wavelength* in that body of theory.

Lacan's inapprehensible, annihilating gaze was streamlined and phallicised by Laura Mulvey in her enormously influential essay 'Visual Pleasure and Narrative Cinema', published in *Screen* in 1975, in which she observed that the conventions of classic Hollywood cinema align the viewer's gaze with that of the fictional male hero with whom the viewer narcissistically identifies, making spectatorship itself a male condition.[101] The male gaze, as if three-dimensional, is directed across the illusory depth 'demanded by the narrative' toward a flat image — a woman, who as 'a cut-out or icon' subverts the reality effect of the conventionally delineated film space. The female movie star is apparently defined by what men think of her: the camera rarely acknowledges her as an active agent by adopting her point of view. Woman, then, is 'image', and man is 'bearer of the look'.[102] This scenario is particularly suggestive of the set-up of *Wavelength*, with its protracted zoom directed toward the 'walking woman' who appears as a flat silhouette or pin-up girl.

The 'walking woman' is certainly a crucial figure among the three images that lure the zoom forward, both as she appears in the double magazine photograph and in two overlapping silhouettes of Snow's own 'walking woman'. Snow has drawn attention to the way that his use of plastics gels as colour filters, crucial to *Wavelength*, originated in two 'walking woman' works, *Morningside Heights* and *Sleeve* (both 1965). One of Snow's notes reads 'Pin-ups — public woman — personal woman — stylised painting', [103] and we can think through some of the functions and the evolution of the 'walking woman' with the help of Merleau-Ponty's meditation on style in art in his essay 'Indirect Language and the Voices of Silence'. [104] Merleau-Ponty understands style not merely as the recognisable external mannerisms that allow us to identify the work of a given painter, but as something profound and inherent in 'the painter's perception as a painter', a deeply experienced meaning for which the painter finds 'the emblems' that will make it accessible to others. [105] One specific example given by Merleau-Ponty reminds us in particular of Snow's 'walking woman':

A woman passing by is not first and foremost a corporeal contour for me, a coloured mannequin, or a spectacle; she is 'an individual, sentimental, sexual expression'. She is a certain manner of being flesh which is given mentirely in her walk or even in the simple shock of her heel on the ground... [106]

In Snow's art practice in the 1960s, the 'walking woman' — especially in works in which she takes the form of a cut-out silhouette through which Snow films other women — seems to incarnate Merleau-Ponty's account of the artist's 'arrangement of certain gaps, or fissures, figures and grounds' to create a 'norm and a deviation in the inaccessible plenum of things'. [107] Most often represented without hands or feet (because she was drawn out of a rectangle), the 'walking woman' implicitly enters into the medium around her, a modern version of the metamorphosis of the mythic Daphne as represented by Bernini, whose finger-tips sprout into the air as leaves as her toes turn into roots.

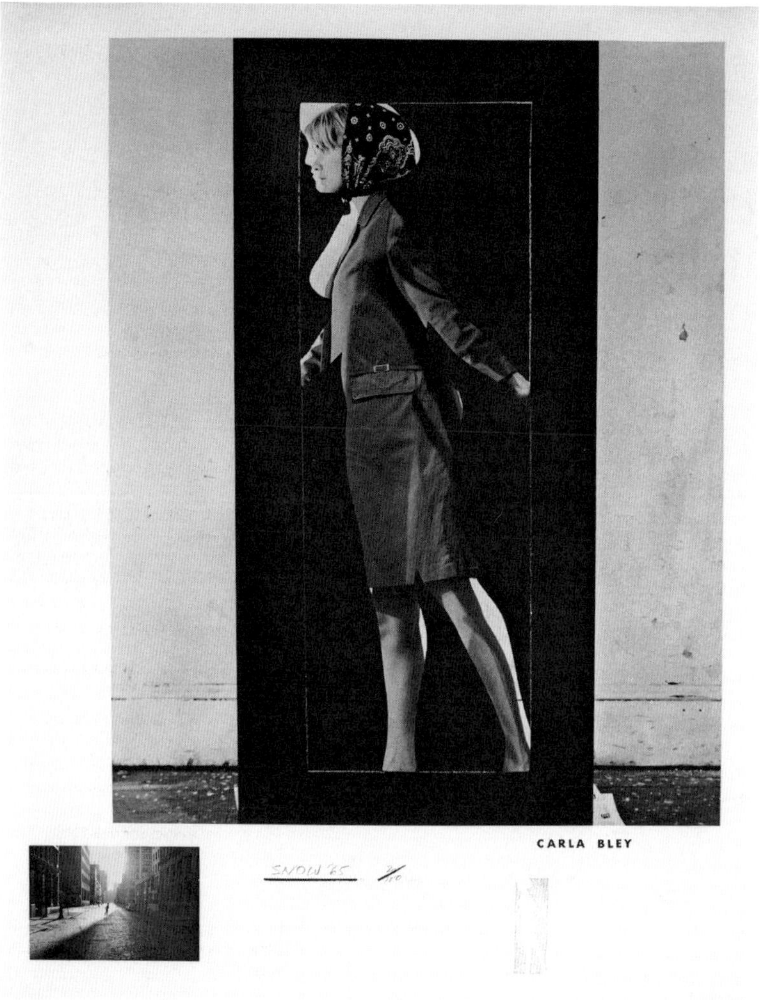

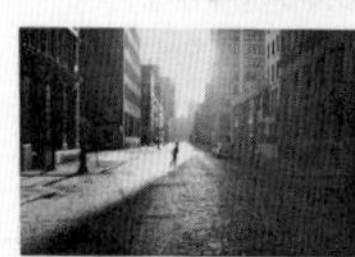

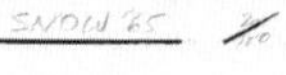

Michael Snow,
Carla Bley, 1965,
offset photolithograph
on wove paper, 66 × 50.8cm
National Gallery of Canada, Ottawa

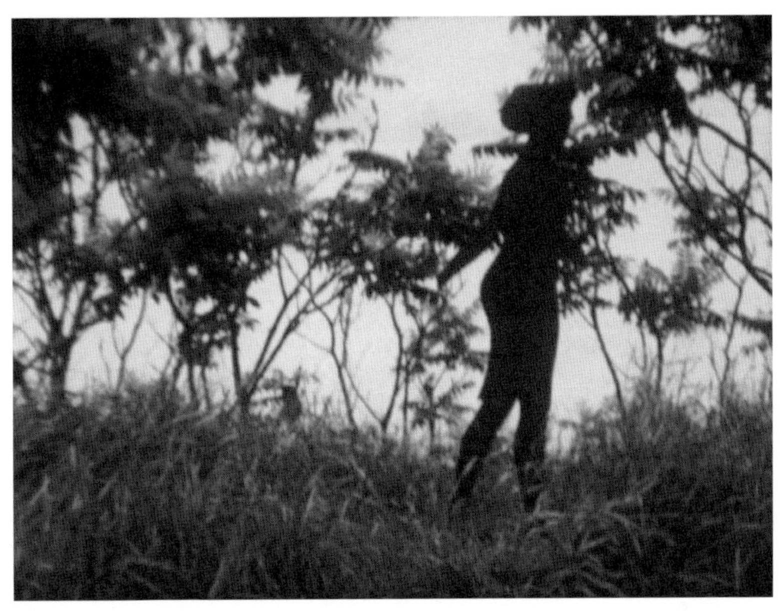

Michael Snow,
New York Eye and Ear Control, 1964,
16mm black-and-white film,
34min, still

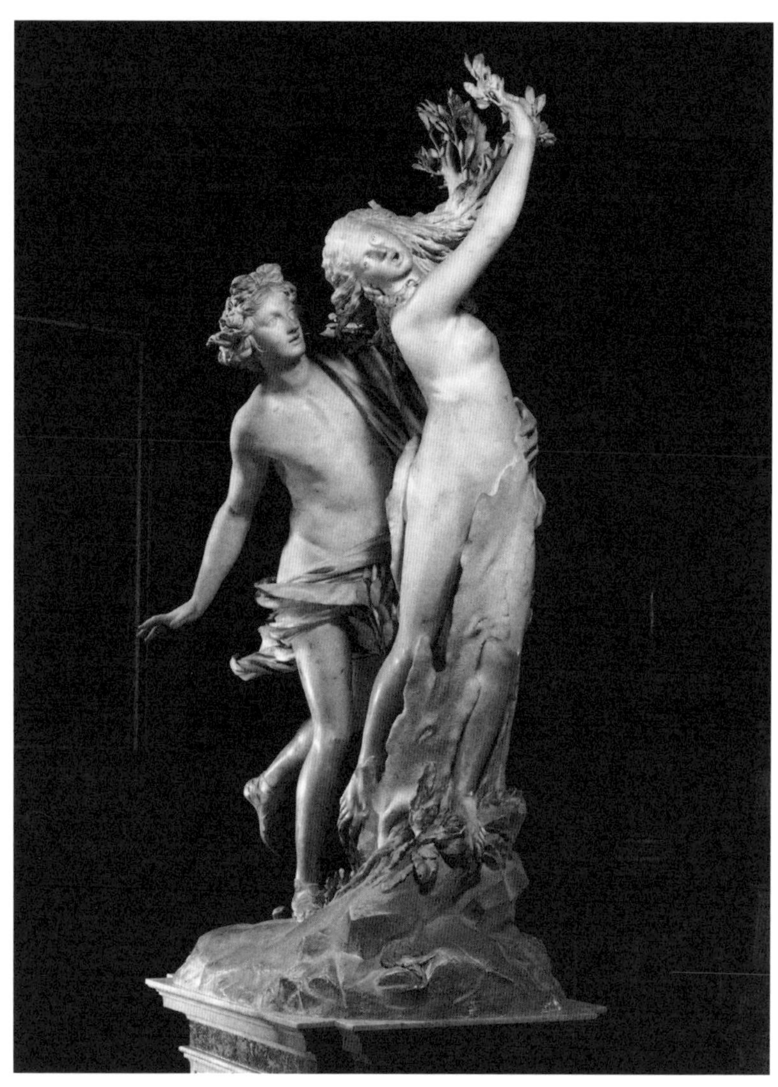

Bernini, *Apollo and Daphne*,
1622—25, marble, 243cm high
Museo e Galleria Borghese, Rome

Miscible in her surroundings, Snow's 'walking woman' can
be understood through the 'chiasmic' moment described by
Merleau-Ponty, in which there is a breakdown of inside and
outside: no longer constrained by the contour of the body,
the viewer is 'caught up in what he sees', not knowing 'which
sees and which is seen'.[108] Merleau-Ponty describes this effect
in terms of the artist who feels himself being looked at by the
things he has painted: 'seduced, captivated and alienated' by this
phantasmic 'outside', he moves into it. Snow's 'walking woman'
can be seen as a sign of this process, and the metamorphic
medium she enters is the vision of others. She 'seduces' by being
seen to be seen. In Merleau-Ponty's account of the figure of the
woman walking by, the woman is both a body walking and a sign
of walking, just as Snow's zoom is a movement into depth and
a flattened equivalent gesture.

It is tempting to see the relations of zoom and 'walking woman'
in *Wavelength* as a precise model for Mulvey's argument.[109] Snow
had specifically considered the kind of space that would seem
'natural' to film — 'maybe conical, but flattened?'[110] — and
from his earliest notes had mused about the zoom as a phallic
'room organ', and the room as 'throat ... canal ... opening'.[111]
This returns us to the vanishing point, which, thought of
as a puncture, was associated with the vagina in Renaissance
theorising on perspective.[112] In one sketch for *Wavelength*,
Snow considered a 'crotch shot' as the zoom's destination —
'something (very small) that you're forced to be very far away
from' — incarnating the perspectival cone as spread legs.[113]
Snow's sketch of a barrier, or 'fence or bars', beside the woman
echoes Albrecht Dürer's famous image of the artist looking
through a pane of gridded glass at — or up — a fore-shortened
reclining nude woman. In this vein, and however unintended
the relationship, George Brecht's Fluxus instructions for timing
a finite but variable ordinary event — say, the time it took for

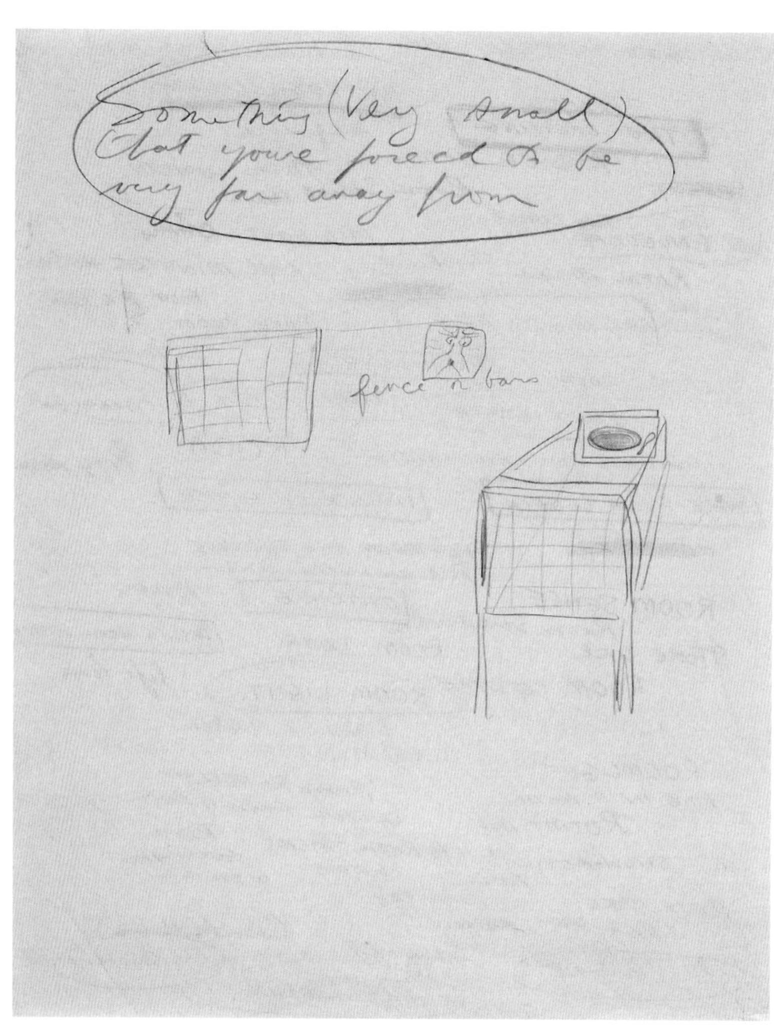

Michael Snow,
sample of notes, 1966.
FS box no.11, file no.3
'Something (very small) that you're
forced to be very far away from'

a candle to burn — find a wittily inflated fulfilment in Snow's
description of the 45-minute running time of *Wavelength*
as 'a nice fuck'.[114]

Annette Michelson also responded to the putatively phallic
thrust of the zoom, converting it into a metaphor of experience
itself, allowing it to become an agent of purification, 'emptying
the space of the film', 'presenting it as mere volume', whose
one, slow movement — characterised by a 'splendid purity' —
is quintessentially philosophical.[115] By dint of Edmund Husserl's
phenomenology, we are kept away from the horizon where the
sexualised vanishing point lodges. Michelson casts the zoom
in terms of Husserl's account of the 'horizon' that marks every
new experience with whatever past knowledge colours our
expectations. Experience allows for an opening up of multiple
potentials for new knowledge as we move through the world,
always approaching a horizon.[116] This might be another
enactment of Zeno's arrow paradox, since, of course, we can
never actually reach the horizon — it is always in retreat,
becoming a new horizon.

The Image in Popular Culture

Less cerebrally, though, the deathly vanishing point was part
of the particularly North American road culture of the 1950s
and 60s. The conception of art as an existential road trip extends
from Jack Kerouac to Hunter S. Thompson, Bob Dylan's *Highway
61 Revisited* (1965) or Tony Smith's account of a joyride on the
New Jersey turnpike. In the February 1967 issue of *ArtNews*,
Allan D'Arcangelo's painting *U.S. Highway 1* (1962), in which
the highway centre line leads to the vanishing point, illustrated
Lawrence Alloway's essay 'Hi-Way Culture: Man at the Wheel'.[117]
In a television commercial for Shell gasoline shown in New York
for several years beginning in 1964, a speeding car tears through
a large white screen. This pop-culture trope can be aligned with

what Stanley Cavell identified as an inherent property of film:
when the world of the moving picture is projected, the screen
actually becomes a *barrier*, keeping the viewer from the world
held within the screen.[118]

What does 'happen' at the vanishing point in *Wavelength*
is a photograph of waves, and it raises questions about the
status of the 'image' at the time. There are a number of ways
of approaching the images on the far wall in *Wavelength*. They
could, hypothetically, be situated within the culture of images
circulating in mass media, as they had been sceptically analysed
in 1961 by the historian Daniel J. Boorstin in *The Image: A Guide
to Pseudo-Events in America*.[119] Especially in the wake of the
assassination of John F. Kennedy and the Warren Commission
Report on his death, there was an aggravated sense of the insuffi-
ciency and ambiguity of visual evidence, fuelling conspiracy
theories. In keeping with the times, in Snow's files we find
a blurb for George C. Thomson's *The Quest for Truth* (1965),
reporting that 'millions of dollars' were being spent to 'suppress'
Thomson's work on the inconsistencies of the Warren Report,
including 'the strange death of Lee Harvey Oswald'.[120] Joyce
Wieland commented in 1964 on the American media obsession
with disasters, the grotesque and 'sensationalism and vulgarity',
as the 'basis of certain kinds of power'.[121] The authentic shocks
and aftershocks of the assassination and the point-blank shooting
of Oswald by Jack Ruby — replayed again and again on television
— contributed to an uneasy sense of something hidden in what
is seen, which could perhaps be retrievable by repeated viewing.
The Warren Commission's enquiry into the assassination was
a miasma of ambiguous and flawed evidence, both auditory and
visual, generating further questions — for example, were there
other assassins, and did the reflections in photographs of the
Texas Book Depository windows capture them? Hollis Frampton
later raised the spectre of the unintelligible reflections and

sightlines that haunted the Kennedy assassination investigation with a glimmer of parodic but still touching paranoia in his film *(nostalgia)* (1971).[122] In it, the narrator recounts the strange case of enlarging a section of a photograph to capture reflected reflections of something ominous but unknown, but the grain of the print obliterates the very details he is trying to make out, and the image remains both dreadful and 'hopelessly ambiguous'. The photographic image that progressively reveals less information as it is enlarged takes us back in cinema history to the disturbing 'little grey smudge' in a wartime aerial reconnaissance photograph that constitutes the moral and literal grey area at the heart of Jean Renoir's *La Grand Illusion* (1937), and forward into the out-of-focus photograph at the end of *Wavelength*. The conclusion of *Wavelength* is possibly the object of Frampton's oblique homage and reversal: whereas the final image of *Wavelength* turns into white light, that of *(nostalgia)* turns into darkness.[123]

In the vein of unreliable images and sinister intents, the recurring post-War trope of the artist as 'solitary, white, male and free' also generates the typical profile of that other American popular cultural icon: the lone assassin.[124] Could the 'sacred studio' loft be transferred to another warehouse, the Texas Book Depository?[125] However tragicomically, could the shifting zoom be taken as an analogy of the assassin's uncertain trajectory? Tom Wolfe wrote about the peculiarity of the *point of view* the media brought to the Kennedy assassination: the camera angles of television, he wrote, have made it seem normal to adopt the viewpoint of the aggressor, of 'Oswald's rifle', of the 'man who is going to strike'.[126] In this ethically suspect situation it is the film viewer, in the cocooning anonymity of the audience, who assumes the role of the assassin. The chimera of the invisible, existential man behind the camera lens or rifle scope also implicates the unseen film director proposed by French

'auteur theory', which was being promoted by Andrew Sarris
in New York film circles at the time.[127] Auteur theory was an
operation of decipherment, the search for the 'recondite motifs'
that defined a given director's work, analogous to a detective's
profiling a criminal through his traces.[128] In Snow's files of
1966 we find the announcement of a public debate, 'Lee Harvey
Oswald: Lone Assassin?', over which Snow stamped his iconic
'walking woman' several times — is she also an assassin?[129]
Certainly, the point of view of the *Wavelength* zoom has been
attributed to her.[130] So we could imagine the point of view of the
zoom as that of the assassin/auteur whom we assemble out of the
visual evidence. Finally, however, the fatality of *Wavelength* is
not lethal — its images are more indeterminate than sinister
— and the popular culture of paranoia does not really provide
the right framework for Snow's waves as 'visible registrars
of invisible forces'.[131]

The Photograph of Waves

Snow gave a lot of thought in his notes to what would be at
the end of the zoom: 'Zoom to what? Why?'[132] His notes suggest
that he thought about different destinations for it, and we could
imagine different implications for each of the destinations:
if the zoom ended at a window, it would then suggest a disappear-
ance at the vanishing point; if a Tom Wesselmann nude, then
the contemporary art scene;[133] if an image of Billie Holiday,
then jazz; if a photograph of a child, then a 'Catholic movie';[134]
if a calendar photograph of Northern Ontario in the autumn,
then the national landscape mythology that defines Canadian
identity.[135] His choice of a photograph of waves has many
implications for thinking about the nature of the photograph
and film still, about seeing, the visible, mortality and, in fact,
for the ways we may think about one image in many different
contexts, testing different points of view.

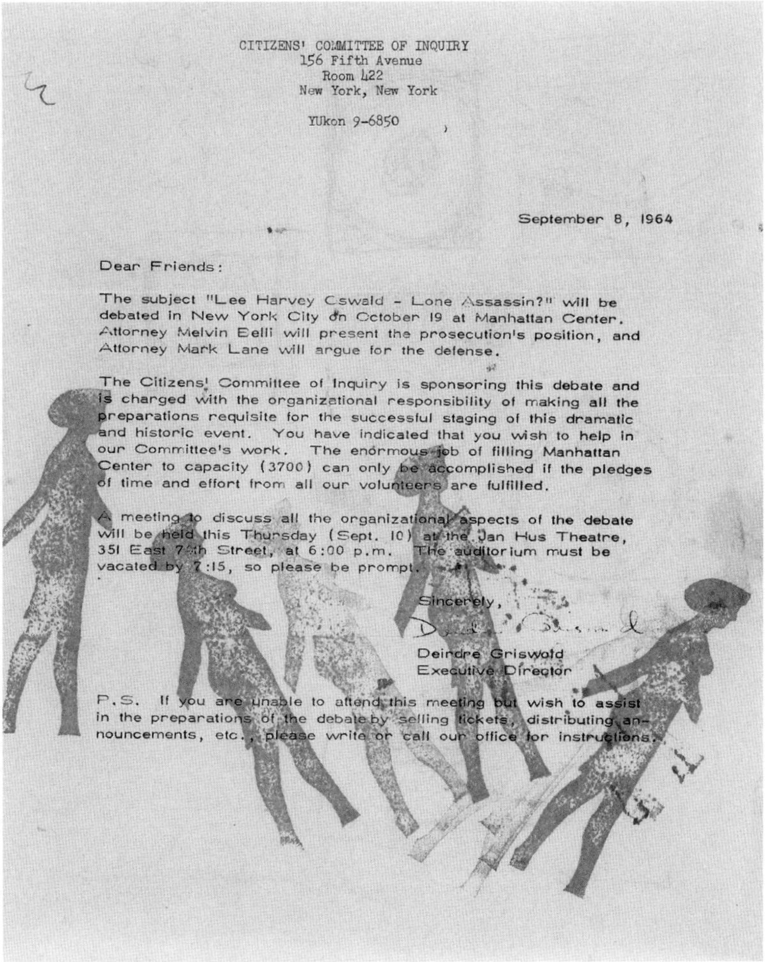

CITIZENS' COMMITTEE OF INQUIRY
156 Fifth Avenue
Room 422
New York, New York

YUkon 9-6850

September 8, 1964

Dear Friends:

The subject "Lee Harvey Oswald - Lone Assassin?" will be debated in New York City on October 19 at Manhattan Center. Attorney Melvin Belli will present the prosecution's position, and Attorney Mark Lane will argue for the defense.

The Citizens' Committee of Inquiry is sponsoring this debate and is charged with the organizational responsibility of making all the preparations requisite for the successful staging of this dramatic and historic event. You have indicated that you wish to help in our Committee's work. The enormous job of filling Manhattan Center to capacity (3700) can only be accomplished if the pledges of time and effort from all our volunteers are fulfilled.

A meeting to discuss all the organizational aspects of the debate will be held this Thursday (Sept. 10) at the Jan Hus Theatre, 351 East 74th Street, at 6:00 p.m. The auditorium must be vacated by 7:15, so please be prompt.

Sincerely,

Deirdre Griswold
Executive Director

P.S. If you are unable to attend this meeting but wish to assist in the preparations of the debate by selling tickets, distributing announcements, etc., please write or call our office for instructions.

Michael Snow,
letter, 1966.
FS box no.11, file no.2

He selected that particular shot out of many photographs he
had taken of the Atlantic ocean because it was not too dramatic
— not too 'splashy' — quite unlike the thirty others taken
at the same time that seem to billow out of, or break against,
the mirroring compartments that frame them in his sculpture
Atlantic (1967).[136] In *Wavelength*, the photograph is projected
over time, making it both film and still, and it concisely touches
on the theorising of photography in film as a series of stills.
The freeze-frame was a device favoured by the *nouvelle vague*,
and the waves of *Wavelength* are a punning nod to this 'new wave',
especially the frozen stare into the camera of the boy by the
seashore at the end of François Truffaut's *Les Quatre Cents Coups*
(1959). Yvonne Rainer dryly ended her *Film about a woman who...*
(1974) with text superimposed on a shot of waves: 'You could
always have an ocean ending. (The image of the ocean fades out.)'

It is as if Snow had tapped into what Siegfried Kracauer identified as 'the continuum of physical existence' in photographs of
waves and machine parts, in which rhythm overrides appearance
and establishes a redundant 'endlessness'.[137] In a way, Snow's
photograph derives enormous traction from stopping that
endlessness: it 'stills' the waves, reminding the viewer of the
stillness beneath film's illusion of motion, the death beneath
the pulse. If, in Kracauer's view, the stillness of a photograph
has a kind of apotropaeic function, in that it fends off fear of
the stillness of death, then, seen up close, Snow's photographed
waves evoke mortality in another way.[138] They form a pattern
of a type that seems to be seen from further away the closer
you move in, becoming an aerial view — very like the close-up
of the wrinkles on Buster Keaton's shut eyelid at the beginning
of Samuel Beckett's *Film* (1965), perhaps proposing analogies
among photographic surface, waves and the webbed patterns
of skin.[139] The eyelid raises the issue of mortality within the
apparatus of seeing, taking the philosophical idea that to see

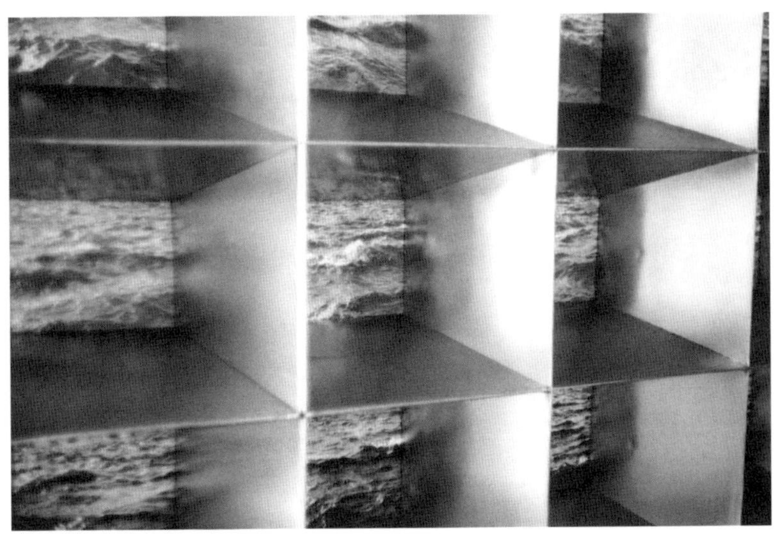

Michael Snow,
Atlantic, 1967,
171.1 × 245.1 × 39.9cm, detail
Art Gallery of Ontario, Toronto

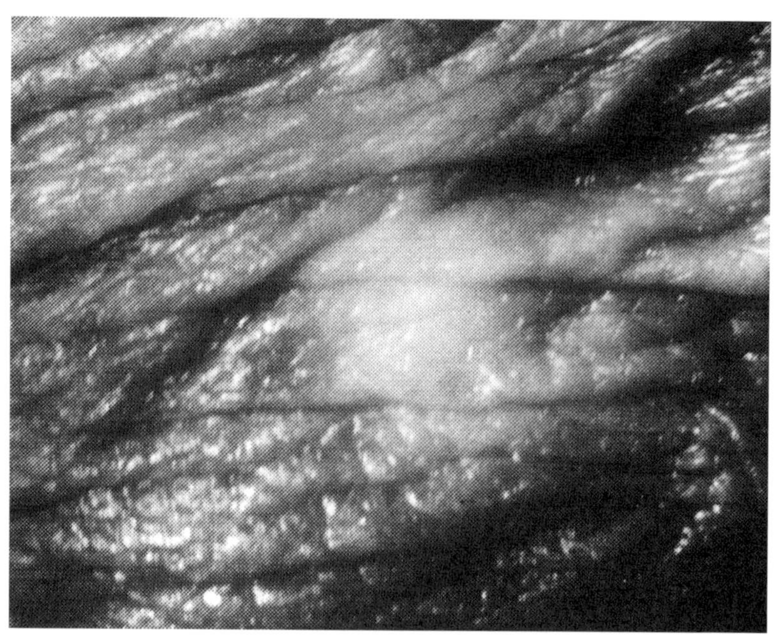

Samuel Beckett,
Film, 1965,
16mm black-and-white film,
24min, still

is to be seen in turn and shifting it to a darker territory — to see
is to be dissolved in the solvent sight of others.

Yet, for a long time, it is not clear that the photograph is
of waves: they appear slightly alien, and might equally be
sedimentary rock, or a glacier, or the surface of a painting.
They necessitate a long, close look and decipherment. In this
way, they may shift the terms to a more profound consideration
of the condition of being visible. Merleau-Ponty had described
the visible as a 'cross-section', or 'surface of a depth', a thin slice
of an unimaginably 'massive being', 'pregnant with texture'.[140]
Snow's image may also be seen as testing and collapsing the
relationship between the represented textures and implicit
depth, subsumed into the triple flatness of photograph, film
and screen. They also raise questions about the relationship
between the ever-smooth photographic surface and the
represented instability of waves. There is a coda to this line
of thinking in Gerhard Richter's book *128 Details from a Picture*,
published at the Nova Scotia College of Art and Design in 1978
and consisting of black-and-white photographs of a painting.[141]
Snow's waves likewise test and collapse the relationship
between the textured material 'content' and the flat photograph
as a metaphor for the thin layer of the visible.

Still and stone-like, as the last thing we come up against in
Wavelength, the waves might invoke Jean-Paul Sartre's example
of a mountain crag as a parable of human freedom.[142] Sartre
points out that the supposed 'resistance' presented by the
'unscalable' crag only exists if we approach the crag as something
that needs to be scaled, but there is 'no obstacle in an absolute
sense'.[143] To a tourist it may constitute 'a pure aesthetic ordering
of the landscape', in which case the crag would not be revealed as
scalable or not scalable, only as beautiful or ugly.[144] Snow's wave
photograph presses the viewer up against the notion of the water

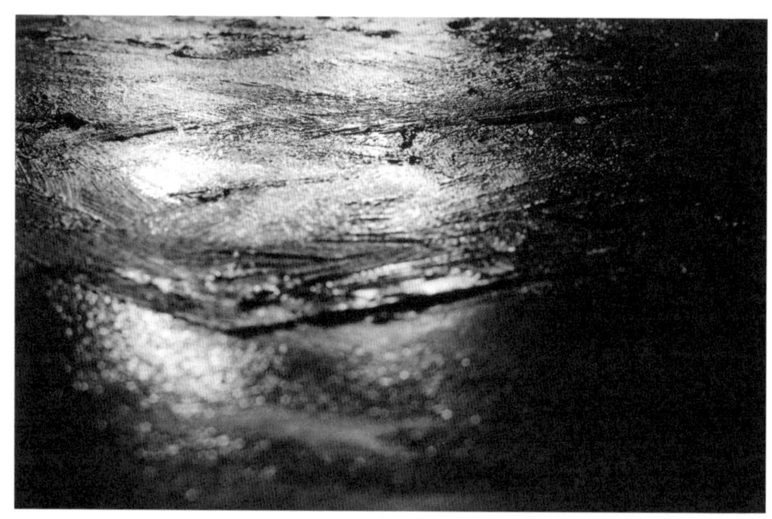

Gerhard Richter,
128 Photos from a Painting, 1998
portfolio containing 8 offset prints,
64.2 × 100.6cm each print,
detail as published in
128 Details from a Picture (Halifax, 1978)
© Gerhard Richter, courtesy
Marian Goodman Gallery, New York

as an obstacle as impassable as the wall on which the image
hangs. At the same time, it is a picture amongst other pictures:
like Sartre's crag, it exists in different situations, presenting
different options for construing it. It might actually constitute
an obstacle — waves that we cannot sail on, or a picture that
we cannot enter. It is framed both by the magazine photograph
of a woman originally understood in a functional, instrumental,
sexual context and by the 'walking woman' — that emblem
of 'the painter's perception as a painter' — in an aesthetic
context.[145] In yet another context, Snow's photograph aligns
with the seashore as a topos of philosophical musing.[146] Paul
Valéry, a poet who had been important to Snow,[147] set a mordant
philosophical dialogue at the edge of the sea in his poem 'L'idée
fixe, ou deux hommes à la mer' (1933), drawing an analogy
between orgasm and life in their shared 'tremendous struggle to
attain a threshold' — which is, in the event, as brief as a sneeze.
The waves, 'vanishing and reappearing', beat out the 'measure
of *infinite* time' as the ironic and inevitable metaphor of that
climax.[148] Snow describes the conclusion of *Wavelength* in
similar terms: 'a "coming" to the final framing. Climax,
that's what I thought.'[149]

After *Wavelength*: ‹—›(*Back and Forth*) and *La Région Centrale*
Wavelength can be taken as the prime object in a series of what
Snow refers to as the 'camera motion' films.[150] If it went
deeply into space while flattening it, his next film, ‹—›(*Back
and Forth*) (1969), unfolded the implications of binary terms
by means of the constant oscillation of a lateral pan, at speeds
ranging from the extremely slow to the vertiginously fast,
punctuated at each limit by a hollow percussive sound that
suggests a predetermined control (although the sounds were
post-synced as part of an exploration of the relations of image
to sound).[151] Snow toyed with events that might echo the pan as
structural binaries, whose differential status is as much erased

as joined by the sweeping movement: a couple embracing, a
janitor sweeping, two men fighting. The camera begins facing
a wall parallel to the picture plane, then pans to the left to a
perspectival view of a classroom. This oscillation picks up speed
until it is a field of energy; at its most intense point, the pans
begin to sweep up and down. All this within the structures of
authority — 1968 was, after all, a year of anti-establishment
riots and strikes in France, the United States and elswhere.
The setting is a classroom, where a man, presumably a professor,
draws a diagram ('<—>') on the board during the slowest part
of the pan. This structural gesture could be taken as shorthand
for an entire intellectual critical apparatus being brokered
in film theory.[152]

The effect of the constant oscillation is not one of equilibrium.
There is a wider arc to the left than to the right, inducing a slight
motion sickness that powerfully reminds the viewer that seeing
is a synaesthetic, whole body experience. Manny Farber described
the film in *Artforum* in particularly virile terms as 'beauty
in ... hardness' and physical labour, and approvingly remarked
on the brawl that followed the first screening of the film at the
Museum of Modern Art in New York.[153] For Farber, the lateral
movement is not only comparable to that of a metronome,
but to a 'guillotine' or a 'butcher's mallet'. He saw the camera's
arcing as solidifying into a sculptural form with 'the hardness,
the dimensions of a concrete beam'. His language — which also
includes the 'jar, jerk, [and] frenetic motion over space' — might
be thought to transform the phallic zoom of *Wavelength* into the
less genteel onanistic counterpart to what Michelson described
as 'rhythmic compulsion and relaxation'. Farber describes the
physiological power of the film, and its testing of experiential
extensions and perceptual limitations. Snow, more meditatively,
has referred to it as a staccato drumming, as opposed to the
lyrical, legato 'song' of *Wavelength*.[154]

The third of Snow's films from around this time to investigate
camera movement and the perception of space is *La Région
Centrale* (1971), a beautiful but not picturesque meditation
on the possible elaborations and limitations of the camera as
'extension' and euphorically untethered 'agent of revelation'.[155]
We have moved from the loft, to the classroom, and then to the
uninhabited — as far as the eye can see — Canadian wilderness.
At three hours, *La Région Centrale* is a very long film, again
'distending' temporality. Snow's comments specifically evoke
Fernand Braudel's *longue durée*, in which time is not scaled to
human history but to the geological or geographical: 'It's 3 hours
long, but it seems like 30,000 years.'[156] Snow designed a machine
with the engineer Pierre Abeloos that held the camera on an
articulated mechanical arm, capable of moving in variable
directions and at different speeds, and of describing spheres.
Concealed behind a large rock during filming, Snow adjusted
a panel controlling the machine. The overall effect is as if the
eye's location were thrown like a ventriloquist's voice, cuing
us to the misdirecting illusions of film movement and sound.[157]
When the camera moves quickly the reverse of field operates:
we experience it as if the landscape — and not the camera —
were moving. This is most striking in the night sequence
in which the moon seems to fling around like a spermatic
tetherball. The soundtrack consists of quiet, electronic beeps,
at a pitch related to the primary direction and speed of the
camera's movement. These punctuating sounds were post-synced
in and they exist in a powerful relationship to the images:
we are not certain whether the beeps 'cause' the camera's
movement, or simply happen at the same time. They have the
cumulatively intense effect of persistence, and they finally
unhinge from the speed of the camera movement in the last
half hour as 'sound and picture come apart' with an ecstatic
force. Snow feels that they function as a 'kind of nervous system'
in the experience of the projected film.[158]

As in *Wavelength*, we are suspended between the sense of an alien world with its own private programme of beeping and movement and the countervailing sense of an immediately present world being intensified for us. While Snow has described the functioning of the camera and machine as 'converging … at the "Nirvanic zero" … the ecstatic centre point completely in 360 degrees … in every direction and *on every plane of a sphere*', in fact the apparatus was designed to *not* film itself, and so did not quite show *every* plane of the sphere.[159] There was a blind spot, as Thierry de Duve points out, perhaps a metaphor for a reflexivity that can take everything but itself into account.[160] This also takes us back to bedevilment of the subject at the vanishing point as it was staked out in *Wavelength*.

One of Snow's recent video installations, *Solar Breath (Northern Caryatids)* (*Souffle solaire (Cariatides du nord)*, 2002) expands *Wavelength*'s peculiar weave of the structural and the lyrical. As in *Wavelength*, we look toward a wall with windows that visually rhymes with the flat plane of the screen. Here, there are two windows, each with a translucent dun-coloured curtain. The window on the left is open, its curtain alternately billowing out and slapping flat — slow or agitated according to the breezes — while the light slowly changes. At one point the curtain before the open window appears as matt greys while the closed window glows golden with the setting sun. The effect is like a visual wind chime. Occasionally we glimpse the northern pine landscape outside, and a table with a solar panel: a reflexive revelation of the power source for the camera and for the image we see — the sun or light itself.

Solar Breath evokes diurnal rhythms, planetary motion and the mythologies of sight and the sun. It could bear out Lévi-Strauss's famous mediation on the relationship of music and myth, in *The Raw and the Cooked* (1964): both need time in order to unfold,

but both also are 'instruments for the obliteration of time'.[161]
Both music and myth operate as stresses between an external
cultural grid and our internal perceptual grid, hollowing out
'momentary lacunae' in the grid of history and elapsed time,
suspending the ordinary temporality in which they take place
to admit us into 'a kind of immortality'.[162] Lévi-Strauss's
metaphor for the temporal effect of music is apposite: 'because
of the internal organisation of the musical work, the act of
listening to it immobilises passing time; it catches and enfolds
it as one catches and enfolds a cloth flapping in the wind'.[163]
Through this metaphor the dun curtain of *Solar Breath* becomes
the fabric of music and mythology. The curtain looks back
to the folds of stretched canvas in Snow's 'walking woman'
sculptures of 1963, *Gone* and *Torso*, which evoke classical
draperies, especially those of the windblown *Nike of Samothrace*.
As the subtitle *(Northern Caryatids)* implies, in *Solar Breath* the
curtain bears the weight of mythologies — of the sun, of nature
and the north — as if a fluttering chiton. It also revisits and
bears out *Wavelength*'s exploration of different registers of time
and of their perceptual suspension.

Wavelength Effects

Wavelength is a lucid, closed-room mystery that evokes and
calls the bluff of the preoccupations of an era. As a 'time
monument', as Snow has also referred to it, it resonates in
other monuments, from Victor Burgin's subtle photographic
and textual renderings of the phenomenological navigation
of the room to the interventions of Richard Serra's steel arcs.[164]
In *Photopath* (1969), Burgin stuck photographs of floorboards,
printed to the actual size of the floorboards, over the floorboards
in question. The images did not align with the original floorboards; rather, they cut across them at a subtle, oblique angle,
in the manner of *Wavelength*'s zoom. As for Serra, who travelled
across Europe showing *Wavelength* — like a phenomenological

Johnny Appleseed — might the reach and slant of the *Wavelength* zoom have inflected his tremendous, resonant steel arcs?

In 1977, Michelson, who promoted Snow's work in France, screened *Wavelength* for Julia Kristeva, at the time an editor of the influential journal of literary and cultural theory *Tel Quel*. Perhaps prompted by the American cultural events in France in conjunction with the United States bicentennial in 1976, *Tel Quel* had declared an ideological 'turn' from Maoism toward an engagement with the cultural production of the United States. Although he was Canadian, Snow, as a key player in Michelson's 'American Independent Film', was represented in the special 'Toward the United States' issue of *Tel Quel* by the translation of a decade-old interview about *Wavelength*.[165] In that special issue, the journal's editors mused on cultural materials received from the United States as if they were raw materials to be worked upon by French dissident intellectuals (that is, themselves).[166] At the time, thinking about sounds, colours and gestures as materials was common within the theorising of theatre and cinema in general. Jacques Derrida had described a new theatre derived from Antonin Artaud's theatre of cruelty, made up of gestures, sounds, cries and lights that would not last beyond the moment of their occurrence.[167] Christian Metz had adapted this to cinema, in which the spectator is made into the delusionally coherent body that apprehends a phantasmic universe of sounds, colours and lights.[168]

Kristeva wrote about *Wavelength* in a separate essay titled 'Modern Theater Does Not Take (A) Place', proposing it as a new 'schizophrenic' theatre of 'sound-colour-gesture'.[169] In this description, she seemingly refracted Snow's own description of *Wavelength* as 'fluctuations of sounds as much as image-colours' and 'waves of colours-images', to relate it to Derrida's account of the theatre of cruelty.[170] (Arguably, though, with its

unaccountable sounds and incidents and colours, Snow's loft
resonates as much with the enchantments of Prospero's island
'full of noises' from Shakespeare's *The Tempest* (1610), as it does
with the lethal, theorised theatre of cruelty gnawing at its own
origins in ritual.) That is, *Wavelength* was implicated as a key
instance of, if not source for, *Tel Quel*'s terms for understanding
the United States. In Kristeva's telling, the zoom becomes
an agent of decay, as objects ebb into a lethal loss of identity,
gradually transmuting the visual field into a final extinguishing
darkness.[171] This concluding darkness, however, was wishful
thinking on Kristeva's part. At the end of the zoom, the waves
lose their texture and cragginess as their contours blur into
something vaguely foetal, but then turn a creamy white:
we are given an auteurial 'snow room'.[172] Snow noted the
recursive temporality of James Joyce's story 'The Dead', which,
like *Wavelength*, loops memory into the present. It, too, ends in
snow: 'falling faintly through the universe and faintly falling,
like the descent of their last end, upon all the living and
the dead'.[173] With respect to this crucial point of the ending,
we could think of the whiteness as having an allegorical
openness, perhaps giving American independent film
something akin to Herman Melville's great American allegory,
Moby Dick (1851):

*Or is it, that as in essence whiteness is not so much a colour as the
visible absence of colour; and at the same time the concrete of all
colours; is it for these reasons that there is such a dumb blankness,
full of meaning, in a wide landscape of snows — a colourless,
all-colour of atheism from which we shrink?*[174]

In all, *Wavelength* reaches beyond its own vanishing point;
and its ambitions and effects — philosophical or pop cultural,
acerbic or nostalgic — seem endless.

FS stands for Fonds Snow, E.P. Taylor Research Library and Archives, Art Gallery
of Ontario. FS documents are listed by box number followed by file number.

1
Michael Snow, 'A Statement on *Wavelength* for the Experimental Film Festival
of Knokke-le-Zoute', *Film Culture*, no.46, Autumn 1967, p.1 (reprinted in Michael
Snow and Louise Dompierre (ed.), *The Collected Writings of Michael Snow*, Waterloo,
Ontario: University of Waterloo, 1994, p.40).

2
FS 11:2.

3
'Theatre — Architecture — Stage lighting — Force People in Frames into Beauty.'
FS 11:2.

4
See also Fred W. McDarrah and Gloria S. McDarrah, *The Artist's World in Pictures:
The New York School*, New York: Shapolsky, 1988; and Alexander Liberman,
The Artist in His Studio, New York: Viking, 1960.

5
Note from March 1963, FS 13:3.

6
M. Snow, 'A Statement on *Wavelength* for the Experimental Film Festival
of Knokke-le-Zoute', *op. cit.*

7
See *George Brecht: Events / Eine Heterospektive / A Heterospective* (exh. cat.),
Cologne: Verlag der Buchhandlung Walther König, 2005.

8
FS 11:2.

9
Conversation with the artist, 25 February 2009.

10
Conversation with the artist, 13 March 2009.

11
FS 11:2.

12
The photograph is of Errol Flynn's last girlfriend, Beverley Aadland, found in
a 'men's magazine'. Conversation with the artist, 7 March 2002.

13
On the misperception that the camera moves, see William C. Wees, 'Prophecy,
Memory and the Zoom: Michael Snow's *Wavelength* Re-Viewed', *Ciné-tracts*,
no.14/15, Summer—Fall 1981, pp.78—83; and Jean Mitry, 'Le Cinéma ou

l'homme imaginaire', *Esthétique et psychologie du cinema*, vol.2, Paris: Éditions Universitaires, 1965, p.29.

14
See Dave Smith, 'Following a Straight Line: La Monte Young', *Contact*, no.18, Winter 1977—78, pp.4—9; and 'Two Evenings of La Monte Young, Tony Conrad, Terry Riley and Marian Zazeela', FS 13:5.

15
Conversation with the artist, 25 May 2009.

16
Originally the sine wave was on a separate quarter-inch tape. The film-maker Jonas Mekas floated the cost of an integrated optical track for the Knokke-le-Zoute competition. Conversation with the artist, 23 March 2009.

17
For a discussion of this 'threshold of tension, of expectation', see Annette Michelson, 'Toward Snow', in P. Adams Sitney (ed.), *The Avant-Garde Film: A Reader of Theory and Criticism*, New York: New York University Press, 1978, p.174.

18
These included Jonas Mekas, Richard Foreman, Amy Taubin, Shirley Clarke, George Kuchar, Ken Jacobs, Nam June Paik and Bob Cowan.

19
M. Snow, 'A Statement on *Wavelength* for the Experimental Film Festival of Knokke-le-Zoute', *op. cit.*

20
Susan Sontag, 'Against Interpretation', *Against Interpretation and Other Essays*, New York: Farrar, Strauss & Giroux, 1966, p.196.

21
Ibid., p.14.

22
See Barbara Rose, 'Looking at American Sculpture', *Artforum*, vol.3, no.5, February 1965, pp.29-36; and 'ABC Art', *Art in America*, October-November 1965, pp.57—69.

23
See B. Rose, 'Looking at American Sculpture', *op. cit.*, p.35.

24
Snow rejects Warhol's 'influence'. FS 2:12. See also Michael Snow, 'Lettre à Thierry de Duve', *Cahiers du musée national d'art moderne*, Autumn 1995, p.107.

25
Annette Michelson, 'Foreword in Three Letters', *Artforum*, vol.10, no.1, September 1971, pp.8—9.

26

On Fried's resistance, see the account of his *Artforum* editor: Philip Lieder,
'An Important World Figure Re-emerges, Unrepentant', *The New York Times*,
3 September 2000, p.3.

27

Indeed, Snow remarks on the flat yellow back of the chair as a plane parallel
to the screen's plane. Conversation with the artist, 19 May 2009.

28

Michael Fried, 'Jules Olitski's New Paintings', *Artforum*, vol.4, no.3, November
1965, p.40.

29

See Annette Michelson, 'About Snow', *October*, vol.8, Spring 1979, p.111.

30

FS 11:2. A yellow chair was part of George Brecht's 'Environments, Situations,
Spaces' at Martha Jackson Gallery (Autumn 1961), and his instructions for 'Chair
Event' (1961) include 'black, spectral colours'. See *George Brecht: Events / Eine
Heterospektive / A Heterospective*, *op. cit.*, p.91.

31

Maurice Merleau-Ponty, 'On the Phenomenology of Language', *Signs* (trans. Richard
C. McCleary), Evanston, IL: Northwestern University Press, 1964, p.94.

32

In relation to the distinction between the distanced 'structural film' and lyricism
as the extension of the body and viewpoint of the film-maker behind the camera
as 'first-person protagonist of the film', see P. Adams Sitney, 'The Lyrical Film',
Visionary Film: The American Avant-garde, 1943—2000, Oxford and New York:
Oxford University Press, 2002, p.160.

33

Letter from the artist to P. Adams Sitney, 1968, FS 11:4.

34

See Bart Testa, 'An Axiomatic Cinema', in Jim Shedden (ed.), *Presence and Absence:
The Films of Michael Snow, 1956—1991*, Toronto: Art Gallery of Ontario and A.A.
Knopf Canada, 1995, pp.35—38; P. Adams Sitney, 'Structural Film', *Film Culture*,
no.47, Summer 1969, pp.1—10 (reprinted in P. Adams Sitney, *Visionary Film*,
op. cit., pp.347—70), and 'The Avant Garde Film: Michael Snow', *Changes*, no.3,
June 1969, pp.15 and 28 (reprinted in *Afterimage*, no.2, Autumn 1970, pp.13—18);
Malcolm Le Grice, 'Thoughts on Recent Underground Film', *Afterimage*, no.4,
Autumn 1972, pp.78—95, and 'Around 1966', *Abstract Film and Beyond*, London:
Studio Vista, 1977, pp.105—23; Annette Michelson, 'Film and the Radical
Aspiration', in P. Adams Sitney (ed.), *The Film Culture Reader*, New York: First
Cooper Square Press, 2000, pp.404—21; and, on *Wavelength* as both politically
subversive and 'epistemological', Gregory T. Taylor, 'The Cognitive in the Service
of Revolutionary Change: Sergei Eisenstein, Michelson, and the Avant-Garde's
Scholarly Aspiration', *Cinema Journal*, vol.31, no.4, Summer 1992, pp.42—59.

35

For the notion of an ontology of film in relation to *Wavelength*, see Peter Gidal, 'Beckett and Others and Art: A System', *Studio International*, vol.188, no.971, November 1974, pp.183—87; and Simon Hartog, 'Knokkenotes', *Cinim*, no.3, Spring 1969, pp.24—26.

36

Michelson argues that Snow only apparently restored the 'transcendental subject' at its centre, in fact subjecting it to constant questioning and qualification. See 'About Snow', *op. cit.*, p.118. In contrast, P. Adams Sitney found in *Wavelength* a romanticism of the 'absolute subject, in all its liberty', in 'The Idea of Morphology', *Film Culture*, no.53/54/55, Spring 1972, pp.1—24.

37

On the analogy between the experience of film and consciousness, see Bruce Elder, 'Michael Snow's *Wavelength*', in Seth Feldman and Joyce Nelson (ed.), *Canadian Film Reader*, Toronto: Peter Martin, 1977, pp.308—23; P. Adams Sitney, 'Introduction', *The American Independent Film*, Boston: Museum of Fine Arts, 1971, pp.1—4; and Stephen Heath, 'Film Performance', *Ciné-tracts*, no.2, Summer 1977, pp.7—17 (reprinted in Stephen Heath ed., *Questions of Cinema*, Bloomington: Indiana University Press, 1981, pp.113—30).

38

In Snow's words: 'You know, what are all these devices and how can you get to see them, instead of just using them?' Scott MacDonald, 'Michael Snow', *A Critical Cinema 2: Interviews with Independent Filmmakers*, Berkeley: University of California Press, 1992, p.63.

39

Manny Farber, 'Film', *Artforum*, vol.8, no.6, February 1970 (reprinted in *Negative Space: Manny Farber on the Movies*, New York: Praeger, 1971, p.250).

40

Postcard from Rainer to Snow, 12 June 1984, FS 5:2. In 1963 Snow received Rainer's call for demonstrations against loft evictions (see newsletter of the Artists Tenants Association, FS 13:5). For the dialectics of *Wavelength*'s abstract and political space, see Michael Sickinski, 'Michael Snow's *Wavelength* and the Space of Dwelling', *Qui Parle*, vol.11, no.2, Fall/Winter 1999, pp.59—88.

41

Email from the artist, 19 October 2005.

42

Marshall McLuhan, *Understanding Media: The Extensions of Man*, New York: New American Library, 1964, p.57.

43

Jorge Luis Borges, 'Death and the Compass', *Labyrinths* (ed. Donald A. Yates and James E. Irby), New York: New Directions, 1962, pp.76—87 (excerpt trans. Donald A. Yates); quoted in Mel Bochner and Robert Smithson, 'The Domain of the Great Bear', *Art Voices*, Autumn 1966, p.41.

44
Apperception was a defining operator in P. Adams Sitney's 'structural' film.
See P. Adams Sitney, *Visionary Film, op. cit.*, p.348.

45
'Letter from Michael Snow' (to P. Adams Sitney and Jonas Mekas), *Film Culture*,
no.46, Fall 1967, p.4.

46
'Converging on *La Région Centrale*: Michael Snow in Conversation with Charlotte
Townsend', in M. Snow and L. Dompierre (ed.), *The Collected Writings of Michael
Snow, op. cit.*, p.59.

47
FS 51:4. Similar terms can be found in Maurice Merleau-Ponty, *Phenomenology
of Perception* (trans. Colin Smith), London: Routledge and Kegan Paul, 1962, p.310.

48
See Gerald Stearn, *McLuhan: Hot and Cool*, New York: Dial Press, 1967, p.199.

49
M. McLuhan, *Understanding Media, op. cit.*, p.299.

50
M. Snow, 'Statement on *Wavelength* for the Experimental Film Festival
of Knokke-le-Zoute', *op. cit.*

51
M. McLuhan, *Understanding Media, op. cit.*, p.358.

52
Letter from Betty F. Lewis to Joyce Wieland Snow, 5 February 1968, FS 11:4.

53
'Infinity Projector', *LIFE*, 2 September 1966, p.64. See also several articles
in the 25 March and 9 September 1966 issues.

54
In *Place des Peaux* (1998), Snow places theatrical gels in thirty suspended
illuminated frames, as scrims for a phenomenological theatre: as the spectator
moves through them, their local and cast colours mix.

55
Snow made a note that read 'Trip Room', FS 11:2. On 'tripping', see Jud Yalkut,
'The Psychedelic Revolution', *Arts Magazine*, vol.41, no.1, November 1966,
pp.22—23.

56
Letter from the artist to P. Adams Sitney, FS 11:4.

57
Timothy Leary, 'She Comes in Colors', *Playboy*, no.153, September 1966 (reprinted in T. Leary, *The Politics of Ecstasy*, London: Paladin, 1970, p.125).

58
Steve Durkee, 'Movie Journals by Jonas Mekas as they Appeared in the *Village Voice*, Subject: Expanded Cinema', *Film Culture*, no.43, Winter 1966, p.11.

59
See Christian Metz, *Le Signifiant imaginaire: Psychanalyse et cinéma*, Paris: Union Général, 1977, pp.64 and 83—86.

60
Jean Mitry, *Esthétique et psychologie du cinéma*, vol.1, Paris: Éditions Universitaires, 1963—65, pp.179 and 182.

61
FS 11:2. 'Day Dream' was used later by Snow in *Rameau's Nephew by Diderot (Thanx to Dennis Young) by Wilma Schoen* (1974).

62
See Viktor Chklovski (Shklovsky), 'L'Art comme procédé', in Tzvetan Todorov (ed.), *Théorie de la littérature*, Paris: Éditions du Seuil, 1965, pp.76—97 (translated as 'Art as Technique', in Lee T. Lemon and Marion J. Reis (ed. and trans.), *Russian Formalist Criticism*, Lincoln: University of Nebraska Press, 1965, pp.3—24.)

63
In the typescript for 'Toward Snow', Michelson changes 'negation of both the continuity and the tension of narrative' to '*distending* the continuity, negating the tension of narrative'.

64
FS 11:2.

65
See Georges Matoré, *L'Espace humain*, Paris: La Colombe, 1962, p.17.

66
See Pamela M. Lee, *Chronophobia: On Time in the Art of the 1960s*, Cambridge, MA and London: The MIT Press, 2004.

67
See Rosalind E. Krauss on temporality in *Wavelength*: 'Dark Glasses and Bifocals: A Book Review', *Artforum*, vol.12, no.9, May 1974, pp.59—62.

68
See Jud Yalkut, '*Wavelength*', *Film Quarterly*, vol.21, no.4, Summer 1968, pp.50—52.

69
See George Kubler, *The Shape of Time: Remarks on the History of Things*, New Haven: Yale University Press, 1962.

70
See Fernand Braudel, *La Méditerranée et le monde méditerranéen à l'époque de Philippe II*, Paris: A. Colin, 1949; or *The Mediterranean and the Mediterranean World in the Age of Philip II* (trans. Siân Reynolds), London: Collins, 1972.

71
See, for example, 'Finished, it's finished, nearly, finished, it must be nearly finished': Samuel Beckett, *Endgame*, New York: Grove Press, 1958, p.1. For Snow's quote, see M. Snow, 'Passage', *Artforum*, vol.10, no.1, September 1971, p.63 (reprinted in M. Snow and L. Dompierre (ed.), *The Collected Writings of Michael Snow, op. cit.*, pp.66—67); and the film script for the 'Hotel Scene' in *Rameau's Nephew by Diderot (Thanx to Dennis Young) by Wilma Schoen* (1974), in M. Snow and L. Dompierre (ed.), *The Collected Writings of Michael Snow, op. cit.*, p.166.

72
Alain Robbe-Grillet, 'Samuel Beckett, or "Presence" in the Theatre' (trans. Barbara Bray), in Martin Esslin (ed.), *Samuel Beckett: A Collection of Critical Essays*, Englewood Cliffs, NJ: Prentice-Hall, 1965, pp.114—15.

73
See Bob Lamberton, '*Wavelength*', *Film Culture*, no.46, Fall 1967, pp.5—6. He characterises the film as 'simple, tragic and inevitable'.

74
S. Hartog, 'Knokkenotes', *op. cit*, p.25. Also raised in Simon Hartog, 'Ten Questions to Michael Snow', *Cinim*, no.3, Spring 1969 (reprinted in Peter Gidal (ed.), *Structural Film Anthology*, London: British Film Institute, 1976, pp.36—37).

75
Steve Reich's typescript, FS 11:4 (reprinted in J. Shadden (ed.), *Presence and Absence, op. cit.*, p.92).

76
A. Michelson, 'Toward Snow', *op. cit.*, p.174.

77
For an overview of system theory, see Ludwig von Bertalanffy, *General System Theory: Foundations, Development, Applications*, New York: Braziller, 1969.

78
See P.M. Lee, *Chronophobia, op. cit.*, p.244.

79
M. McLuhan, *Understanding Media, op. cit.*, p.358.

80
For Snow's quote, see S. MacDonald, 'Michael Snow', *op. cit.*, p.67. For structuralist accounts of narrative, see, for example, P. Gidal, *Structural Film Anthology, op. cit.*; and P. Adams Sitney, 'Structural Film', *op. cit.*

81
On a reading of *Wavelength* in relation to Robbe-Grillet, see Dominique Noguez,
'On *Wavelength*', in *Michael Snow* (exh. cat.), Lucerne: Kunstmuseum Luzern, 1979,
pp.93—108, especially p.102; and Adele Freedman, 'The Disappearing Man',
Canadian Art, vol.11, no.1, Spring 1994, p.37.

82
Roland Barthes, 'Introduction à l'analyse structurale du récit', *Communications*,
no.8, 1966, pp.1—27 (translated as 'Introduction to the Structural Analysis of
Narratives', *Image-Music-Text* (ed. and trans. Stephen Heath), London: Fontana
Collins, 1977, pp.79—124).

83
FS 11:2.

84
Sigfried Giedion, *Space, Time and Architecture: The Growth of a New Tradition*,
Cambridge, MA and London: Harvard University Press, 1941, p.760.

85
M. Merleau-Ponty, *Phenomenology of Perception*, *op. cit.*, p.265.

86
See Edmund Carpenter and M. McLuhan, 'Acoustic Space', in Edmund Carpenter
and Marshall McLuhan (ed.), *Explorations in Communication: An Anthology*,
Boston: Beacon Press, 1960, p.67.

87
'Letter from Michael Snow', *op. cit.*, p.5. Snow is key in Maria Walsh's argument
for a hybrid spectator, neither deluded or ensnared, on the one hand, nor constituted
as the phenomenological 'transcendent subject' or ego, on the other. See Maria
Walsh, 'The Immersive Spectator: A Phenomenological Hybrid', *Angelaki*, vol.9,
no.3, December 2004, pp.169—85.

88
See Michael Fried, 'Art and Objecthood', *Artforum*, vol.5, no.10, June 1967,
pp.19—20.

89
'Letter from Michael Snow', *op. cit.*, p.5.

90
FS 11:2.

91
See G. Kubler, *The Shape of Time*, *op. cit.*, p.18.

92
Robert Rauschenberg, 'Random Order', *Location*, vol.1, no.1, Spring 1963,
pp.27—32; quoted in Rosalind E. Krauss, 'Perpetual Inventory', *October*, vol.88,
Spring 1999, p.97.

93
Robert Smithson, 'Untitled (Air Terminal — Windows)' (1967), in Jack Flam (ed.), *Robert Smithson: The Collected Writings*, Berkeley: University of California Press, 1996, p.356.

94
On de Saint Phalle, see *LIFE*, 1 April 1966, pp.58—60; and *Art News*, vol.65, no.3, May 1966, pp.14—20. See also Klaus R. Scherpe and Brent O. Peterson, 'Dramatization and De-Dramatization of "The End": The Apocalyptic Consciousness of Modernity and Post-Modernity', *Cultural Critique*, no.5, Winter 1986—1987, p.128.

95
M. Merleau-Ponty, *Phenomenology of Perception*, *op. cit.*, p.364.

96
Hollis Frampton, 'Incisions in History/Segments of Eternity', *Artforum*, vol.13, no.2, October 1974, p.40.

97
See Joe Medjuck, 'The Life and Times of Michael Snow', *Take One*, vol.3, no.3, January—February 1971, p.9; and 'Conversation with Michael Snow', *Film Culture*, no.46, Fall 1967, pp.1 and 3—4.

98
Jacques Lacan, *The Four Fundamental Concepts of Psychoanalysis* (ed. Jacques-Alain Miller, trans. Alan Sheridan), New York: Norton, 1998, p.83.

99
Ibid., pp.92—93.

100
See, for example, Jean-Louis Baudry, 'Ideological Effects of the Basic Cinematographic Apparatus' (trans. Alan Williams), *Film Quarterly*, vol.28, no.2, Winter 1974—75, pp.39—47; and Christian Metz, *The Imaginary Signifier: Psychoanalysis and the Cinema* (trans. Celia Britton, Annwyl Williams, Ben Brewster and Alfred Guzzetti), Bloomington: Indiana University Press, 1982, p.14.

101
See Laura Mulvey, 'Visual Pleasure and Narrative Cinema', *Screen*, vol.16, no.3, Autumn 1975, pp.6—18. For Snow on Mulvey, see S. MacDonald, 'Michael Snow', *op. cit.*

102
L. Mulvey, 'Visual Pleasure and Narrative Cinema', *op. cit.*, p.12.

103
FS 11:2.

104
M. Merleau-Ponty, 'Indirect Language and the Voices of Silence', *Signs*, *op. cit.*

105
Ibid., p.53.

106
Ibid.

107
Ibid.

108
Maurice Merleau-Ponty, 'The Intertwining: The Chiasm', *The Visible and the Invisible: Followed by Working Notes* (ed. Claude Lefort, trans. Alphonso Lingis), Evanston, IL: Northwestern University Press, 1968, p.139.

109
Stephen Heath recognised the influence of *Wavelength* on the 'disframing' in Laura Mulvey and Peter Wollen's film *Penthesilea* (1974). Stephen Heath, 'Narrative Space', *Screen*, vol.17, no.3, Autumn 1976, p.107.

110
'Conversation with Michael Snow', *op. cit.*, p.3.

111
FS 11:2.

112
See Donald Keith Hedrick, 'The Ideology of Ornament: Alberti and the Erotics of Renaissance Urban Design', *Word and Image*, vol.3, no.1, January/March 1987, pp.111—37.

113
FS 11:2.

114
S. Hartog, 'Ten Questions to Michael Snow', *op. cit.*, p.36.

115
A. Michelson, 'Toward Snow', *op. cit.*, pp.174—75.

116
See Edmund Husserl, *The Paris Lectures* (trans. Peter Koestenbaum), Hague: Nijhoff, 1967, p.32; quoted in A. Michelson, 'Scène de l'action espace du mouvement: La crise de la réprésentation cinématographique', in Peter Kubelka (ed.), *Une Histoire du cinéma* (exh. cat.), Paris: Centre Georges Pompidou, Musée national d'art moderne, 1976, p.43. Gilles Deleuze responded to the Husserlian terms set by Michelson in *Cinéma 1: L'Image-mouvement*, Paris: Éditions du Minuit, 1983, p.177.

117
Lawrence Alloway, 'Hi-Way Culture: Man at the Wheel', *Arts Magazine*, vol.41, no.4, February 1967, pp.28—33.

118
Stanley Cavell, 'It screens that world that it holds from me', *The World Viewed: Reflections on the Ontology of Film*, New York: Viking Press, 1971, p.24.

119
Daniel J. Boorstin, *The Image: A Guide to Pseudo-Event in America*, New York: Vintage, 1987, p.6.

120
FS 13:5.

121
Jonathan Holstein, 'New York's Vitality a Tonic for Canadian Artists', *Canadian Art*, issue 93, vol.21, no.5, September/October 1964, p.278.

122
See Rachel Moore, *Hollis Frampton: (nostalgia)*, London: Afterall Books, 2006, p.48.

123
Snow was the narrator of *(nostalgia)*; see S. MacDonald, 'Michael Snow', *op. cit.*, p.61—62. Snow, like Frampton, denied any relationship to the move into a photograph that takes place in Antonioni's *Blow Up* (1966). 'Evening with Michael Snow', Museum of Modern Art archive, 'Cine-Probe' Series, sound recording #D69.18 1969.

124
For a discussion of the tropes of the artist in *his* studio, see Caroline Jones, *Machine in the Studio: Constructing the Postwar American Artist*, Chicago: University of Chicago Press, 1996, p.57; Marcia Brennan, *Modernism's Masculine Subjects: Matisse, the New York School, and Post-Painterly Abstraction*, Cambridge, MA and London: The MIT Press, 2004; and Michael Leja, *Reframing Abstract Expressionism: Subjectivity and Painting in the 1940s*, New Haven: Yale University Press, 1993.

125
FS 11:2.

126
Tom Wolfe, '(Intermission): Pause, now, and consider some tentative conclusions about porno-violence: What it is and where it comes from and who put the hair on the walls', *Esquire*, vol.68, no.1, July 1967, p.110.

127
See, for example, Andrew Sarris, 'Notes on the Auteur Theory', *Film Culture*, no.27, Winter 1962—63, p.1; and 'The American Cinema', *Film Culture*, no.28, Spring 1963, p.1.

128
Peter Wollen, 'The Auteur Theory', in Leo Braudy and Marshall Coen (ed.), *Film Theory and Criticism: Introductory Readings*, Oxford, London and New York: Oxford University Press, 1999, pp.519—35.

129
Snow was aware of the cultural impact of John F. Kennedy's assassination. See
announcement of a debate between Marvin Belli (the lawyer for Jack Ruby) and
Mark Lane, in a letter from the 'Citizen's Committee of Inquiry', 8 September 1964,
FS 13:6. Snow gives mock crossword clues, 'A young president and his wife'
and 'Alleged assassin', in 'Ten Artists in Search of Canadian Art', *Canadian Art*,
issue 100, vol.23, no.1, January 1966, p.62.

130
At least by P. Adams Sitney, in 'The Implications of Michael Snow's Cinema',
typescript (Anthology Film Archives, New York), p.10.

131
'Conversation with Michael Snow', *op. cit.*, pp.4—5. More apposite is Paul Valéry's
account of Leonardo da Vinci: 'Today there are still lines of force traversing all
space, but one can no longer see them. Might they perhaps be heard? It is only
the mental flights suggested by melodies that can give us some idea of intuition
of trajectories in space-time. A sustained note represents a point.' Paul Valéry,
'Introduction to the Method of Leonardo da Vinci', *The Collected Works of Paul
Valéry* (ed. Jackson Mathews, trans. W.M. Stewart), Princeton: Princeton
University Press, 1971, vol.8, p.58.

132
FS 11:2.

133
See Green Gallery invitation with Wesselmann's *Bathtub 3* (1963), FS 13:6.

134
FS 11:2. Snow's phrases ('fruit of thy room', 'holy wave length' and 'holy room
data') allude to the traditional iconography of the Annunciation to the Virgin
Mary, a 'ROMB ROOM ZOMB ZOOM WOMB', fertilised by the waves of light
and sound ('room ray', 'room egg', 'room beam').

135
FS 11:2.

136
Conversation with the artist, 3 April 2008.

137
Siegfried Kracauer, *Theory of Film: The Redemption of Physical Reality*, London,
Oxford and New York: Oxford University Press, 1978, pp.63—65 and 71.

138
See Siegfried Kracauer, 'Photography' (trans. Thomas Y. Levin), *Critical Inquiry*,
vol.19, no.3, Spring 1993, p.433.

139
Snow refers to *Film* (1965) in his notes. FS 11:3.

140
M. Merleau-Ponty, *The Visible and the Invisible*, *op. cit.*, pp.134—36.

141
Gerhard Richter, *128 Details from a Picture*, Halifax: Nova Scotia College
of Art and Design, 1978. Snow's book *Cover to Cover* (1975) was also published
by the NSCAD press. It is tempting to think of Richter establishing a dialogue
with Snow's work after his visits to NSCAD.

142
Jean-Paul Sartre, *Being and Nothingness* (trans. Hazel Barnes), New York:
Washington Square, 1966, p.620.

143
Ibid., p.627.

144
Ibid.

145
M. Merleau-Ponty, 'Indirect Language and the Voices of Silence', *op. cit.*, p.53.

146
See, for example, Søren Kierkegaard, 'One Must Have Doubted', *Philosophical
Fragments* (ed. and trans. Howard V. Hong and Edna H. Hong), Princeton:
Princeton University Press, 1985, p.159; or Friedrich Nietzsche, *Daybreak* (trans.
R. J. Hollingdale), Cambridge and New York: Cambridge University Press, 1982.

147
On Valéry's early importance to Snow in the 1950s, see Elizabeth Kilbourn,
Michael Snow: Retrospective 1965 (exh. cat.), Toronto: Isaacs Gallery, 1965.

148
Paul Valéry, 'L'Idée fixe, ou deux hommes à la mer', *The Collected Works of Paul
Valéry*, *op. cit.*, vol.4, pp.10—11 and 27.

149
Email from the artist, 19 October 2005.

150
Snow's 'camera motion' films are *Wavelength* (1967, zoom), *Back and Forth*
(1969, panning), *Standard Time* (1967, circular panning), *La Région Centrale* (1971,
spherical panning), *Breakfast (Table Top Dolly)* (1972/76, dollying), *Presents* (1980,
trucking of set, hand-held pans) and *Seated Figures* (1988, trucking).

151
The percussive sounds were made by lining up black leader film with the edited
film in a synchroniser, and then cutting a V-shaped notch out of the edge of the
black leader wherever the pan reached one end or the other of the picture; when
the notched film was 'played' in a 16mm projector with the sound-head on, it made
the sound that happens at the end of each pan as each notch passed the optical lamp.
The 'mechanical' sound was made by what Snow calls a 'metal thingme [*sic*] that got

dinged by a revolving metal part of this projector [...] All the voices were recorded
separately and then these three elements were mixed to a final recording (16mm
magnetic tape) from which the optical track was made'. Email from the artist,
27 May 2009.

152
See Michael O'Pray, 'Framing Snow', *Afterimage*, no.11, Winter 1982—83,
pp.51—65.

153
See M. Farber, 'Film', *op. cit.*, p.84.

154
Email from the artist, 25 May 2009.

155
FS 10:3.

156
Ibid.

157
See Rick Altman, 'Moving Lips: Cinema as Ventriloquism', *Yale French Studies*,
no.60, 1980, pp.67—79

158
With a sound technician, they constructed an instrument similar to a synthesizer,
with which it was possible to control pitches and the rate of beeps. Snow and
Abeloos realised that making a sound program to control the movements of the
camera-bearing machine would be possible, but too time-consuming. Consequently,
the sound-instruction idea was the model for what was actually post-synced.
Email from the artist, 27 May 2009.

159
FS 10:4.

160
See Thierry de Duve, 'Michael Snow: The Deictics of Experience and Beyond',
Parachute, no.78, April/May/June 1995, p.34.

161
Claude Lévi-Strauss, 'Overture', *The Raw and the Cooked* (trans. John Weightman
and Doreen Weightman), Chicago: University of Chicago Press, 1983, p.16.

162
Ibid., p.27.

163
Ibid., p.16.

164
M. Snow, 'Statement on *Wavelength* for the Experimental Film Festival
of Knokke-le-Zoute', *op. cit.*

165
Michael Snow, 'Lettre et conversation', *Tel Quel*, no.71—73, Autumn 1977,
pp.237—46 (originally published in English as 'Conversation with Michael Snow',
op. cit.)

166
See Julia Kristeva, Marcelin Pleynet and Philippe Sollers, 'Pourquoi les Etats-
Unis?', *Tel Quel*, no.71—73, Autumn 1977, pp.3—20 (translated as 'The U.S. Now:
A Conversation' (trans. Phoebe Cohen), *October*, vol.6, Autumn 1978, pp.3—17).

167
See Jacques Derrida, 'The Theater of Cruelty and the Closure of Representation',
Writing and Difference (trans. Alan Bass), Chicago: University of Chicago Press,
1978, pp.232—50, and especially pp.40—41.

168
See C. Metz, *The Imaginary Signifier*, *op. cit.*

169
Julia Kristeva, 'Le Théâtre moderne n'a pas lieu', *Trente-quatre/Quarante-quatre:
Cahiers de recherche des sciences des textes et documents*, no.3, Winter 1977, pp.13—16
(translated as 'Modern Theater Does Not Take (A) Place' (trans. Alice Jardine and
Thomas Gora), *SubStance*, no.18/19, 1978, pp.131—34).

170
For Snow, 'Letter', in *Michael Snow: Sept films et plus tard* (exh. cat.), Paris: Centre
Georges Pompidou, Musée national d'art moderne, 1977 (translated from *Film
Culture*, no.46, Autumn 1967, pp.4—5). For Derrida, see 'Theater of Cruelty', *op. cit.*,
pp.240—41 and 246.

171
See J. Kristeva, 'Le Théâtre moderne n'a pas lieu', *op. cit.*, p.14.

172
FS 11:2.

173
Snow linked a looping conversation that 'repeats and ends up where it started'
with 'The Dead', FS 13:3. James Joyce, 'The Dead', *The Dubliners*, Project Gutenberg,
1 September 2001, available at http://www.gutenberg.org/dirs/etext01/
dblnr11h.htm (last accessed on 11 June 2009).

174
Herman Melville, *Moby Dick, or the Whale*, Evanston, IL: Northwestern University
Press, 1988, p.195.